AWAKENED LEADERS

EMPOWERING STORIES OF SELF-HEALING, TRIUMPH AND TRANSFORMATION

COMPILED BY AERIOL ASCHER
#1 INTERNATIONAL BEST SELLING AUTHOR

Awakened Leaders
Empowering Stories of Self-Healing, Triumph and Transformation

Copyright © 2022 by Aeriol Ascher

Aeriol Publishing, BodyMindSoul TV & Media Network
San Jose, CA.

All rights reserved. No part of this publication may be reproduced distributed or transmitted in any form or by any means including photocopying recording or other electronic or mechanical means without proper written permission of author or publisher, except in the case of brief quotations embodied in critical reviews and certain other noncommercial uses permitted by copyright law.

ISBN 979-8-9860274-0-1 (paperback)
ISBN 979-8-9860274-1-8 (hardcover)

Visit us on line at **www.AeriolAscher.com, www.BodyMIndSoul.TV**
Printed in the United States of America.

WHAT PEOPLE ARE SAYING

"Just what the doctor ordered"
—**Maureen Ryan Blake**, Founder of The Power of the Tribe

"Read and be inspired!"
—**Andrea Lewis**, Writer, Poet, and Essayist

"Embrace your full leadership potential."
—**Rebecca Hall Gruyter**, Empowerment Leader and CEO of RHG Media Productions

"A blend of compelling stories infused with tips and techniques that elevate the soul for optimal healing and joyous living."
—**Heather Larkin**, Author, Owner, KC Holistic Healing

"Certain to help shift the consciousness of our planet through their stories, insights and wisdom."
—**Wendy Lee Baldwin Hargett**, Author and Personal Growth Mentor

"This book will transform your life."
—**Linda Lenore**, M.A. Feng Shui Master, Award-Winning Speaker, and Author

"I found myself feeling encouraged, aware, and understood."
—**Shelby Kottemann**, Author, Speaker, and Healer

"Readers will no doubt find circumstances to which they can relate and guidance that will help them find peace and powerfully leave their mark on our world."
—**Amy Riley**, Keynote Speaker, #1 International Best-Selling Author, Consultant, and Coach

"Rise like the phoenix and stand in your power to make an impact on generations to come."
—**Linda Joy Benn**, Transformational Catalyst, Founder of the Benn Method™

"An amazing collection of stories that inspires you to break free and embrace your own leadership"
—**Seema Giri**, Author, Speaker, Mentor, and Founder of Uplyft Media

ACKNOWLEDGEMENTS

I want to acknowledge myself for being the visionary and leader behind BodyMindSoul.TV and Media Network and committing to supporting the voices of healing by producing, publishing, and bringing forward meaningful media which both empowers individuals and raises the consciousness of the planet.

I would like to thank my grandma, Lela Weiland, may she rest in peace. She planted a seed in me to always write my story down.

I would also like to thank my mom, Carole Ascher, who I know loves me all the way to Pluto and back, and without whose generous sponsorship these publishing projects would not be possible.

I want to thank Rebecca Hall Gruyter and the RHG Publishing team for diligently assisting me in bringing these publishing projects into fruition.

Of course, I would also like to express my deep gratitude to each of the co-authors. Thank you for hearing and answering the call. These Awakened Leaders have poured their hearts and loving essence into this project in order to give you perspective, perseverance, and hope for a brighter future. I hope you are as inspired by their beautiful stories as I am.

Thank you to our BodyMindSoul.TV & Media Network sponsors for your support in making all our educational programing and the enlightening interview series *Positive Vibes* possible.

Thank you to the subscribers of the *Positive Vibes with Aeriol* podcast and the Voice America TV show where we are *Healing Body Mind and Soul* by empowering all souls in need with expert advice on self-care, self-healing, and self-mastery with our programming and empowering interviews with top experts in the field of holistic healing, personal development, and transformation.

And thank you to you, our dear reader. Thanks for picking up this book! Thank you for opening your mind, opening your heart, and striving to embody your most masterful self for a better world. May you be touched, moved, and inspired by the stories of these Awakened Leaders. May you be empowered to achieve success beyond your wildest dreams, may your heart be filled with joy, and may you find everlasting peace profound.

Do what makes your heart sing!

Aeriol

CONTENTS

Introduction 9

Part One - Our Evolving World 13

    Balancing our World with Feminine Leadership By Paula Pacheco 15
    The Power of Leading with Self-Love By Anna Brooke 25
    Freedom from Fear By Beth Proudfoot, LMT 33
    Music in My Head By Holly Chadwick 41
    Finding Peace Profound By Aeriol Ascher 49

Part Two - Building a Legacy 57

    One Decision Can Change Your Life By April Shoemaker 59
    The Transformative Power of Family By Diana Pohle, PhD 67
    The Art of Relationship By Laura Schoolcraft 75
    Building Connection with Unlikely Companions By Julia Harriet 85
    Touched by Love from the Other Side By Alan Grenwoolf 91

Part Three - Change in Action 99

    How I Became the Goddess of Joy By Robyn Vie Carpenter 101
    Owning my Leadership Story By Dr. Beth Halbert 109
    Journey Towards Wholeness By Riya Wang 117
    From Caregiver to CEO By Helen Miller-Montana 127
    Empowered Recovery and the Dance of Life
    By Cathlene Michaels-Brader and Matthew Noonan 139

Closing Thoughts 147

Reviews 149

About BodyMindSoul.TV Network 153

Aeriol Publishing 155

INTRODUCTION

Dear Reader,

Thank you so much for leaning into our powerful book.

I was extremely humbled by the success that our last book project at BodyMindSoul.TV & Media Network produced and the amazing milestones that *Empowered Self-Care: Healing Body, Mind, and Soul for a Better World* reached. Some of those precious milestone achievements included:

1. Two 2020 Communicator Awards of Distinction from the Academy of Interactive and Visual Arts for podcast show hosting and also for our branded podcast series *Self-Care Under Quarantine* during the pandemic lockdown.

2. *Empowered Self-Care: Healing Body, Mind, and Soul for a Better World* became a bestseller in fifty-six categories across five countries. Twenty-one of those reached the #1 position on Amazon during our launch in February 2021.

3. In May 2021, our speaker community won another Communicator Award of Distinction for our video series *The Empowered Self-Care Book Talk Series*.

4. And we also won a Silver Visionary Award from the Coalition of Visionary Resources for the same video series, *The Empowered Self-Care Book Talk Series*.

I was blown away at what we had co-created, and, if I am perfectly honest, which I usually am, I was a little intimidated to follow up a project like that, to say the least! Where the previous book had basically presented itself to me, this one felt like it was teasing me forward and testing my resolve in my business as a communicator and as a leader.

The book mission revealed itself to me slowly at first and was informed by the feedback I had received from the previous anthology. The readers by far commented the most on how much they loved the stories. Not the modalities, not even the free gifts or expert tips. What the readers loved the most were the heartfelt and inspiring accounts of the personal healing journeys of the authors themselves. And so our mission, title, and objective became clear.

The Awakened Leaders Book Mission

The purpose of the *Awakened Leaders* book is to raise the consciousness of the planet by empowering as many people as possible. By stepping forward as Awakened Leaders, we offer hope, inspiration, and guidance to others as we evolve into more enlightened ways of being and more purposeful ways of living. By sharing our stories of self-healing, triumph, and transformation, we hope to empower others to live to their highest potential and overcome any seeming obstacles in their path. It is our belief that by co-creating our Awakened Leaders book project as a collective, we can reach, inspire and empower the most people and, in doing so, raise consciousness and heal the planet itself.

As I further felt into our Awakened Leaders book project, soon the book cover artwork started slowly revealing itself to me. At first, a keyhole-shaped "portal" through which the collective wisdom of the group could unlock new states of consciousness was the inspiring vision that was driving me forward into the project. Finally I arrived at the somewhat surreal image you find on our book cover. It represented so many aspects of what I felt was necessary to usher in light, hope, and new states of awakened consciousness onto the planet. I hope it is thought-provoking and speaks to your journey and the steps we take towards enlightenment and awakened consciousness.

One by one, I started connecting with the authors who would eventually form our collective. By the time our Awakened Leader co-author group was finally formed, it did not take long before I knew we had achieved what we had set out to do. We had gathered these sixteen amazing leaders, transformational coaches, spiritual teachers, and self-healing guides to share their amazing tales of victory over the slings and arrows of everyday life and how they transcended their own limitations and oppression to resiliently rise above limiting circumstances to a life that thrives.

Without further ado, I invite you to step into this book with an open mind and an open heart to receive the wisdom of these Awakened Leaders. We hope to inspire you on your own personal self-healing journey, the journey towards your own awakened self-leadership. It is our hope that you will shift and expand your definition of what self-healing and leadership means to you and that you will awaken an awareness of your own divinity that drives you forward in your life with passion and purpose.

To your success!

Aeriol Ascher

Please watch our Awakened Leaders Book Talk Series on YouTube

PART ONE

OUR EVOLVING WORLD

"Never doubt that a small group of thoughtful, concerned citizens can change the world. Indeed it is the only thing that ever has."
—Margaret Mead

BALANCING OUR WORLD WITH FEMININE LEADERSHIP
BY PAULA PACHECO

We Live in a World of Duality

Divine Feminine energy was up on Mount Olympus looking down on the Earth that she had just created. She was awed by just how beautiful the Earth was. She loved it like a mother. She immediately flew down and entered into the earth, and she became Mother Earth. (From a fable.)

Earth was created in perfect balance through the concept of duality. Duality teaches us that every part of life has a *balanced* opposite part or complementary interaction. Good/Evil, Black/White, Love/Hate, Up/Down are examples of duality in this world.

Within each human being resides the duality of our Feminine and Masculine energies. The Divine Feminine is one half, and the Divine Masculine is its complementary interaction. When in balance together, these two energies create a beautiful world filled with love, harmony, and peace. Human beings therefore can also live a life filled with love, harmony, and peace. But this is not the world we find ourselves in today.[1]

Divine Feminine energy is nurturing, patient, intuitive, gentle, full of wisdom, with a receiving nature. Divine Masculine energy is logical, strong, loyal, action-oriented, adventurous and has a giving nature. These are only a few of both of their energies.[2]

In its truest, brightest form, the Divine Masculine has great integrity. This energy is courageous, intellectual, and grounded. It is nonjudgmental, independent, and mindful.

When balanced, the Divine Masculine energy perfectly matches the Divine Feminine in its brightest and truest form. One would think with all of these wonderful and magnificent energies we have available to us, life on the Earth would be spectacular. Well, why isn't it?

To everyone's detriment, masculine energies have *dominated* our world for a millennium. Society has placed so little value on feminine energies that both energies are now terribly out of balance. One can easily see this imbalance just by seeing how out of balance the world is today.[3]

Due to this imbalance, masculine energies have become aggressive, controlling, and frighteningly abusive. It is an energy that never stops hungering for more power, more dominance, and absolute control. We have wars, strife, riots, poverty, and food shortages all over the Earth. We also have people holding dominion over other human beings, as well as patriarchal structures that disempower so many human beings.

The Divine Masculine that we see today is a toxic version of its true, glorious energy, full of strength and protecting ways. In many places around the world, women suffer because of this great imbalance and are oppressed and violated daily. This toxic masculine energy can also be seen in the patriarchal systems and societies that run our world.

---

[1] *Embracing the Feminine Nature of the Divine* by Toni G. Boehm, PhD. Inner Visioning Press, 2001.
[2] *Embracing the Feminine Nature of the Divine* by Toni G. Boehm, PhD. Inner Visioning Press, 2001.
[3] *Feminine Masculine Balance: A Paradigm Shift for a Peaceful and Abundant Society* by Jacqueline McLeod. Lioncrest Publishing, 2018.

There are also people who are unbalanced in their Divine Feminine energy and can be recognized because they engage in toxic communication with others. They think that femininity makes them weak, and they have a great need to prove themselves. They are always busy doing instead of being. Add to that, our feminine energies have traditionally been so devalued that many women are prone to continue to feel stressed and struggle all the more with confusion and chaos.4

When both of these energies are balanced, we experience a greater sense of harmony and fulfillment in our lives. The healthy goal is to create a balance in your masculine and feminine energies, because it can also help improve so many other aspects of your life, especially your physical, emotional and spiritual well-being. It all comes back to the duality of balancing the Divine Feminine and Divine Masculine energies.

But have faith, the Divine Feminine is coming out of the shadows, and she is on the rise. This energy is slowly waking up and returning to us all. Women and men around the world are hearing her call. It is awakening after a forced slumber of at least 2,000 years.

What Is the Divine Feminine?

The Divine Feminine is an energy, which means it can't be seen or heard, but it can be *felt*. It is the feminine energy that exists in all living beings on Earth, including the ocean, moon, trees, planets, and just about everything. This energy is sometimes known as Yin energy, Shakti, Kali, Gaia,5 and Mother Earth.

In its truest nature, the Divine Feminine energy is loving, nurturing, motherly energy and empowered from within. It also exudes beauty, sensuality, and attraction. This energy can also be called on to offer creativity and inspiration in its purest form. When in balance, peace and harmony surround this energy.

This energy speaks of abundance in all things and the knowing that the Earth will always provide enough. It is an energy that is intuitive and fully

---

[4] *Divine Feminine Handbook: Overcoming Self-Doubt* by Marilyn Pabon. Balboa Press, 2021.
[5] https://www.gaia.com/article/goddess-gaia

open to receive whatever is necessary for the health of the Earth and all of its inhabitants.

It is energy that is also wild, free, and untamed. Societies' unwritten rules and boundaries, constructed to keep this feminine energy caged, she dismisses with a wave of her hand. This energy rises above and makes a path of her own.

Unafraid to speak truth or embrace its sexual nature, this energy shows up fully and authentically. Her intuition can always be a trusted guide. Existing in the cyclic rhythm of the moon and the seasons is a way this energy finds balance. Understanding the sacredness of all life, this energy trusts that all needs will be met.

I have just described the true nature of a person who is most comfortable exhibiting more of their Divine Feminine energies. Even if this doesn't resonate with the person you are today, the Divine Feminine is still there within you, waiting patiently to connect with you, be embraced and welcomed by you.

How We Lost Our Connection to the Divine Feminine

I read that at the dawn of civilization, the first early village communities that came together were centered around women. Women were revered and respected. Women were honored as priestesses of the Divine Feminine. They had this status because women not only birthed the species, they also bled but did not die. Seen as sacred, women were the first tribal leaders, healers, and spiritual advisors. History calls these matriarchal societies.[6]

Archaeological evidence shows that these matriarchal societies had no defenses except those used to protect against wild animals. There were no weapons found. The bodies in the gravesites that were found bore no traces of violence. That said, one could surmise that people in these communities resolved conflict through peaceful ways, and the society was relatively balanced in terms of the feminine and masculine.[7]

---

[6] *Feminine Masculine Balance: A Paradigm Shift for a Peaceful and Abundant Society* by Jacqueline McLeod. Lioncrest Publishing, 2018.
[7] *Feminine Masculine Balance: A Paradigm Shift for a Peaceful and Abundant Society*, by Jacqueline McLeod. Lioncrest Publishing, 2018.

In these matriarchal societies, art and culture flourished, life and the Earth were considered sacred, revered, and to be honored. According to one school of thought, around 12,000 years ago matriarchal societies ended when farming began and people started to settle down. Once weapons were developed for defense, the power shifted to the physically stronger male. Female autonomy ended. Patriarchy was born.

For the past few thousand years, the Divine Feminine energy has been repressed and cast away but not forgotten, never forgotten. The Divine Feminine had to hide from this unbalanced Divine Masculine because it didn't have a safe place to fully express itself and its energies here on Earth. The Divine Feminine has been hidden away in the hearts and minds of many, just waiting for the right moment to come back when most needed.

In 2011, I was taking a class at Stanford University. The subject was Women's Leadership. I walked in and sat down with eighty other women. One of the two instructors began the class by saying, "Ladies, the Divine Feminine is back!"

In my head, I did a happy dance! After the shock of hearing one of the finest educational institutions in the world affirm Her presence back on the planet, I smiled all day long and for weeks to come.

If you have found your way to this article, chances are *you* have heard her call. I hope you are ready to explore how to awaken the Divine Feminine waiting patiently inside of you to help heal ourselves and our planet.

Awakening the Divine Feminine

Deep down, we all feel an imbalance in our lives brought on by the imbalance of Mother Earth. But most of us don't know what that is or what a solution even looks like. We live in our minds, disconnected from our bodies and our emotions. We are hungering to make that connection with her, the Divine Feminine.

Over the past hundred years, the women's movement has sought to address these imbalances by putting more women in leadership positions, fighting the wage gap, and—of prime importance—holding men accountable for their abuse of girls, boys, and women. Worthy endeavors to be sure.

But the patriarchy will only go so far in allowing these changes to succeed. We must begin to create real transformation in our world. Real transformation must start with the people that believe in the dire need for the Divine Feminine to emerge. If men and women still do not welcome or respect the Divine Feminine energies, then the imbalance will remain.

The ultimate goal, of course, is for the Divine Feminine to sit beside the Divine Masculine and work together as equals to save the planet. That is the only way we can survive as a species. There is much education needed to awaken us all to the chaos we create and live in and guide us back to our true, whole selves as caretakers of each other and of Earth.

Despite the natural resistance to change that comes with being human, the Divine Feminine is still rising. The Divine Feminine does not care if it will be welcomed with open arms. The Divine Feminine has come back now because humankind is at the precipice of the climate change disaster. This feminine energy has been reflecting, learning, and growing in the shadows all this time. It is that feminine *energy* that is what many women and men are beginning to feel as a collective.

It is that feminine strength—along with masculine strength, standing up together—that is causing huge disruptions to our world. A longed-for breakdown is beginning to occur of outdated patriarchal systems.

It is that united strength that is causing the breakdown of old beliefs whose time has long passed. These beliefs are being replaced with goals of real equality, compassionate treatment of animals, ethical and sustainable living choices. More decisions being made for the collective instead of the wealthy.

Oh *yes*, She is rising. Are you ready to rise with her? If Divine Feminine energy speaks to you and you want to call her qualities into your life, it begins with awakening the Divine Feminine within you.

Below are just some of the ways to awaken this energy within you. On my website I have posted a list of Divine Feminine and Divine Masculine energies.

Because this is *energy*, you might be a little confused about how to begin. So here are some practical ways to awaken this energy inside of you. The information below can help us to make space for the vibration of the Divine Feminine to rise within us and show up fully.

Steps to Awakening the Divine Feminine Within You

1. Love Yourself Exactly As You Are.

If we haven't yet learned to fully love ourselves, how can we show real love and compassion for anyone around us? Learn to have genuine compassion for all living things. Stop comparing yourself to others, because we always fall short. We can always find something about ourselves we just don't like.

Remember that a divine spark lit up and you were uniquely created. You are so unique that there is not a single human being on Earth that is like you. You can love yourself for that reason alone!

2. Connect With Your Body in Ways That Are Healing For You.

Many of us hold great amounts of trauma, stress, and abuse in our bodies. This energy can stay stuck there. Don't let the pressure of the constant media-critiquing and body-shaming decide for you what your body should look like.

Try body-healing therapies like breathwork and massage. Learn about self-care practices. Try moving your body through yoga, stretching, running, and walking.

Yoga is a great way to learn how to be fully present in the world. Just moving your body helps connect you. Being fully present has many outstanding benefits. It can increase memory, focus, and it can reduce stress.

3. Use Your Incredible Intuition As Often As Possible. Intuition is one of the most powerful qualities you can use, not only at work but in all of your daily interactions. Do not use your intuition when you are emotional but when you are calm and relaxed.

At work, your intuition helps you to sense when things are off or realize the true purpose of an assignment and get to the goal quicker. It also helps you become more open to new ideas.

4. Access Your Creativity. This quality can be useful in every area of your life. You can more easily:

Use your intuition to make better decisions

Connect more with your body

Work with your inner guidance and trust more often

Use your creative energy to problem-solve

Be fully open to receive new ideas and solutions

Be able to be fully present in the moment

5. Visit Nature. Spending more time in nature will help you feel more connected to the Divine Feminine and her beautiful oceans, blissful fresh air, and magnificent mountains.

6. Speak Your Truth. Women are so used to being hushed, or having their ideas ignored. When we keep out mouths shut and hide our truth, we are blocking the Divine Feminine wisdom that wants to express herself.

We have the power to embrace and express the Divine Feminine and Divine Masculine energies within us. We can act with compassion, promote peace, live in abundance, nurture ourselves and our Earth, and slow down so we can live a richer, fuller life.

The Divine Feminine and the Divine Masculine can help us save our planet, returning peace and harmony to it. We have to awaken these energies within ourselves first.

My website discusses the above steps about awakening the Divine Feminine and goes into more detail regarding the feminine and masculine energies.

Paula Pacheco

At the age of fourteen, Paula walked into the kitchen where her mother was teaching one of her sisters how to cook Chicken Marengo, a favorite family dish. Her mother asked her if she wanted to learn how to make the dish. She politely told her mother no thank you, that she was going to be a corporate businesswoman and wouldn't need to know how to cook. In spite of not knowing where that thought had come from, it just felt so right. In that exact moment, Paula knew what her professional goal was going to be.

In 1994, Paula received a BA in liberal studies with a concentration in consulting organizational development, as well as a certificate in business consulting psychology from John F. Kennedy University in Orinda, California. Additionally, she attended the following schools:

- Stanford University, Stanford, CA, eight professional business development courses, 2011–2014

- UC Berkeley, Berkeley, CA, certificate in business process management, 2013

Paula has an accomplished, diverse corporate operational background that includes Fortune 500 companies such as Bank of America, IBM, PGE, the Pacific Stock Exchange, the entertainment industry, the nonprofit sector, high-tech startups, and the construction industry.

When asked once what does she do, she responded, "I fix operational situations, problems, and changes. My expertise is in business process management, developmental change, analyzing, managing, growing, training, and restructuring business operations."

Paula has traveled to Chicago and Dallas on business, as well as been to Canada and to Europe twice on vacation.

Paula is now working on creating workshops that will help women succeed in corporate leadership by utilizing their inner skills and talents. Paula still doesn't care to cook.

www.paulapacheco.com
paula@paulapacheco.com

THE POWER OF LEADING WITH SELF-LOVE
BY ANNA BROOKE

I grew up in New York City, so I like to think of the many bridges there as a metaphor. We used to drive across the George Washington Bridge, a huge expanse across the Hudson River, and often get stuck in traffic along with hundreds if not thousands of other cars and trucks. I would hate when we stopped on the bridge, because I could feel the bridge itself bounce in response to the thousands of tons barreling back and forth across it. The first time I experienced it, I froze in terror. My mom, seeing me, told me that the bouncing was a sign of how strong the bridge was. The beams were responding to the stress of the weight by redistributing it, hence the waves we felt. The bridge's ability to respond is what defined its very stability. Even though it still felt uncomfortable, I was able to relax and trust that we were going to make it across safely.

How does the bridge handle such constant, incredible weight and stay standing? In short, I'd say good engineering that allows stress to be safely distributed and good materials that provide the resilience to do so.

What does this look like if we apply it to ourselves? Where are we conducting connections, either as leaders or simply as humans? Where are we resilient, and where is there room to improve our ability to respond to everyday challenges big and small?

What I want to share with you is this—you can build resiliency by facing challenges with more self-kindness and gentle reminders that it's okay to be uncomfortable, because in that discomfort is great learning.

So how do you respond to a challenge? How do you talk to yourself? Do you take care of yourself in the process? Upon resolution, do you tend to feel depleted, neutral, or ready for more? What would change if you brought in kindness, self-care, and steady support and encouragement for yourself?

A teacher of mine once broke the word *responsibility* down into "the ability to respond." If as leaders we do not cultivate our ability to respond to stress, breakage can occur, whether in our composure or communication. If we have developed coping strategies to disperse stress more effectively, we find increased resilience as a natural byproduct of their use. It may not mean that challenges get any easier, but by having in place a framework to take care of ourselves amidst the stress, we are able to tap into increasingly larger amounts of potential and peace.

I felt like a natural-born leader from day one. I am the first child and only daughter of my parents, which may well have predisposed me to confident delegation and an innate sense of leadership. I was class president, actively involved in every school play, and even started an initiative to get my school cafeteria to stop using styrofoam. My mother says that I was loud in my opinions and mostly right. In addition to being recognized for my young leadership and initiative, I was also constantly told that I was bossy. This didn't stop me from having an innate knowledge of how to run the show, but words like *bossy*, *loud*, and *self-centered* had a ruinous effect on my confidence. It changed how I chose to show up in the world. I had no resources I could fall back on and was not able to respond to what felt like cannonballs and spears from others. The judgment got louder and louder as I went through school and entered my early twenties, and the stress of it broke something inside of me. My confidence felt permanently dented, and I had no sense of my worth. I learned to hide my own voice in favor of lifting others' and strengthened the mask I wore so as to stay safe from other people's opinions of me.

I learned that even though my self-confidence was exceptionally low, I could put on a good show. I benefit from a lot of privilege, including having a body that is white, pretty, slender, and tall. Because of it, I was never challenged and knew nothing of resilience. I confused appearance with value and my body with my worth. It was a dysfunction that seemed implicitly normal, as I saw examples of these binaries all around me. I also loved performing, and there was something very comfortable about it. Beauty was very easy to perform, even if I felt empty. Without a healthy outlet, however, a lot of that creative energy became pent up and started to become self-destructive.

I have since learned that my worth is not defined by what I look like or what scenes I have access to. I know and trust that I am lovable exactly as I am simply by virtue of being alive. I don't have to do anything to be loved, and I don't have to listen to the opinions of others when I know what needs to be done and how. I am enough, just as you are enough exactly as you are, with gifts and challenges alike.

So now comes the fun part. I want to share three tips that have helped me immensely and that I hope will support you in making peace with your own power and help you remember that you can always choose to lead from a place of love.

I want to start this by saying that I feel we have a responsibility to ourselves to tell the truth. When we tell ourselves the truth faster, we can embrace change in the tides of movement and new possibilities that come with it. This may not necessarily be a comfortable experience, but it is an expedient one. My healing brought me into the heart of my truth, and I realized I could set down all the masks and negative self-belief that I had accumulated over the years and say yes to my vision and dreams.

I always wanted to be in the spotlight, on the microphone, or the master of ceremonies. Saying yes to that dream led me home into my purpose and my empowerment. I started dancing, producing shows, and stepping into the shoes of a full-time entertainer while also being a teacher and healing arts facilitator. I love helping others to recognize their own inner purpose and longing and helping them clear the path to their own empowerment. I would not have been able to do this if I had not first done it for myself.

Tip one: Tell yourself "I am still learning" whenever you are on a steep learning curve, no matter the lesson.

Navigating the harder, more uncomfortable emotions can feel like a very steep learning curve. Wading through fear, shame, and judgment in order to rise through challenges is rarely comfortable. However, it is made more comfortable, more human, when I remind myself (sometimes out loud) that I am still learning.

When we affirm we are still learning, it softens judgment around any expectation of perfection and reminds us that we are acquiring insight and understanding one very human step at a time. It helps to put failures into perspective, shifting them from what might feel like a disaster into a learning experience. Are you going to be mad at a fifth-grader for being in fifth grade? Of course not. So why be hard on yourself when in fact you are just still learning?

Tip two: Learn to sit with discomfort.

Moving through tough emotions is neither pleasant nor comfortable, but, as many therapist friends of mine say, the only way out is through.

Our nerves are our personal electrical systems, and when we practice sitting with discomfort, we give ourselves the opportunity to cultivate powerful personal insight while developing resilience in our nervous system. Is it comfortable? Rarely. But what can emerge is a new flexibility and compassion as we build our resilience. No one is perfect, and everyone messes up. Sitting with discomfort is a way to digest the electric charges of fear, shame, or judgment that can surge up in us when we get triggered or confronted with any harm we have received, caused, or participated in. When I realized how much harm I had inflicted on those around me (and myself) by clinging to my abysmal sense of self-worth, I had to sit for a good long time in order to fully digest and understand my role and how it all played out. It was immensely uncomfortable, but I made it through, and so can you.

We are beginning to see what happens when systems designed to oppress, control, and condition us are challenged with the light of truth, equity, and fairness. So, what happens when we start to look at how we subscribe to and obey these systems? It is essential that we learn to sit with the results of our own choices and actions so that we can consciously change them and make new choices. Sitting with discomfort is a practice of holding the parts of ourselves that we haven't yet learned how to hold with love. Whether asking for forgiveness or owning our role in whatever caused harm, we build emotional strength and fluency that allows for increased clarity and connection with others.

Tip three: Practice self-care whenever and wherever you can.

You have likely heard this thousands of times, but I cannot stress this enough. When we develop and practice the reflex to regularly care for ourselves, we build a more defined sense of what feels good and what doesn't. From this place of discernment, we get to establish our own boundaries and make choices from a place of self-ownership.

Relationships are our best teachers. The example I'm going to give here is a personal one regarding a tumultuous and fraught love relationship I had years ago. After years of feeling pushed and pulled, I made a firm choice to love myself more than a guy who was running roughshod all over my heart. I vowed from that point on to love and care for myself first and foremost. It shifted my perspective forever, and I began to trust my gut no matter what. It was as if my heart had said, "Yes! You finally chose me! Let's do this!" It didn't prevent future heartbreak, but that decision created a baseline that helped me trust myself and my resilience. That one choice—to love myself no matter what—was a major game-changer for me rooted in the transformational power of self-love, which is the essence of self-care.

One note of importance here: there is a big difference between self-soothing and self-care. These two things are often confused for one another, and they do hold similarities, but there are also distinct differences. Self-soothing is any comforting behavior that helps us to calm down and times of stress. Examples include taking a warm bath, binge-watching your favorite TV series, and eating delicious chocolate if some hard stuff has happened. These are just a few ways that we can feel comforted and soothed in the moment, lowering our stress response and creating more comfort in the body, but it's not a permanent solution to the root cause. Self-care is essential if we are to educate ourselves into change through our own love. And the biggest canvas we have to practice self-care on is ourselves and our bodies.

One of the biggest frontiers of change that is leading the way on the rising tide of self-love is the reclaiming of the inherent value and sacredness of bodies in all their shapes, sizes, ages, abilities, cultures, and heritages. What would it look like for you to take good care of your body as a way to liberate and reclaim yourself from any doubt of your innate worth?

I believe we are in a time of emergence where old systems are showing cracks and breaking down. We all carry traces of these systems in us and our nerves and bodies. What if personal, radical, consistent self-care is what begins to break the attachments we hold and systems that benefit few and hurt many? What if we made a choice to educate ageism, racism, ableism, and size-ism out of our bodies? What if each of us started with loosening any attachment to the systems that have created immense harm in our lives and histories as a way to lead? What if we each chose love as our priority and practiced leading our lives from there?

The choice to love is a brave one. When we choose to lead with love, we open up myriad possibilities to change, grow, and evolve. Look back at the tips I just shared, because they all lead to this. Normalizing learning curves and the inevitable discomfort that comes with leading our lives are two gifts we can give ourselves in the name of adaptation, versatility, and exploration. They are not called "growing pains" for nothing, and we can settle the charge arising from discomfort by anchoring down into caring for ourselves. In doing so, we practice becoming a source of meeting our own needs, which in itself builds resilience and strength.

I like to think of the whole of humanity as an enormous disco ball, with each of us a single mirrored tessera reflecting our unique light out into the universe. Each of us is brilliant in our own way, and I wonder what life would look like if we each got out of our own way and allowed our incredible light to shine freely and widely.

The choice to love yourself no matter what is the ultimate form of self-care. What could our world look like if everyone started to care for themselves in ways that help them feel nurtured and supported? What would happen to short tempers, or overcrowded schedules, or mixed priorities that create confusion and stress? What if everyone took exceptionally good care of themselves so that they could more brilliantly and steadily shine their point of light out into the universe in their own perfect way?

The choice is yours, and I encourage you to step forward, to make your magic happen, and create new conduits of possibility in your life and the world. Caring for yourself as you navigate where life takes you is a profound act of claiming your worth and showing those around you that self-care can become a natural part of the decision-making process. Take the steps you need to be able to more readily respond to stress or challenge, and in doing so you will build your strength and stability. Powerful leadership begins in the heart and radiates outward. I hope you cultivate the willingness to become the source of making loving choices for yourself, for others, for community, and for humanity. In doing so, you will show others that they can do it too. What else makes a good leader?

Anna Brooke

Anna Brooke is an interdisciplinary healing arts practitioner and the author of *Stripped Down: How Burlesque Led Me Home*. She is also known as Rev. Legs Malone, a burlesque performer, show producer, educator, and advocate of all things striptease who has been featured in Page Six, Buzzfeed, and Huffington Post.

She has taught her transformational classes since 2010 all over the world, most notably at BurlyCon (www.burlycon.org), the world's only burlesque educational convention. Anna became a wedding officiant in 2016, thus incorporating Reverend in her stage name. It is her goal to help people reconnect with their own essence in love and discover deep, soulful possibilities in their lives.

www.annabrookehealing.com
facebook.com/annabrookehealing
instagram.com/annabrookehealing

FREEDOM FROM FEAR
BY BETH PROUDFOOT, LMT

Growing up in California, we often had "duck-and-cover" drills at school. In case of an earthquake, we were supposed to scooch under our little desks and huddle with our hands over our necks until the roof stopped falling. This created the illusion of safety. We had the shields of our little desks. We knew what to do. As I grew, though, I discovered that earthquakes strike when you least expect them, and there is rarely a shield in sight when they do.

I had just turned fifty years old when my husband of twenty-seven years came to me and said, "I want a divorce. I don't love you anymore. I haven't loved you for a long time."

My legs gave way. I know very well, and knew then, that this made me look incredibly foolish. But it was true that if you had asked me the day before, I would have told you that I was sure that my husband loved me.

Apparently, I was either naïve or incredibly stupid, and my life had been a lie. I couldn't trust my intuition about people, so there was no one I could trust. And I was losing the man I'd come to in times of distress for my entire adult life, so I felt I was all alone in a suddenly dangerous world. I spiraled down into a dizzying and dark place. The first time my husband had the kids for the weekend after he'd moved out, I sat down on the couch and wept and didn't get up until my sister called, and I had to crawl to the phone. "How long has it been since you've eaten?" she asked. I couldn't remember.

My sister was a dynamo. She decided I needed to be rescued, and she took the job seriously, forcing me to eat, to exercise, to talk about it. I had so many conflicting emotions, I thought I might drown in them. And she kept pulling me to the surface and pushing me to get the help I needed.

One afternoon, we were hiking, and I became suddenly dizzy. I had to sit down before I fell.

"That's weird," my sister said.

"I'm okay," I said. "It's just my body reflecting my inner reality. There is no floor beneath my feet."

"Nope," she said. "You need to call your doctor about this."

Well, I was in the middle of the negotiations for my divorce, being assaulted daily with decisions I had no idea how to make, emotions that were cycling through so fast I found myself crying in the line at Safeway. And I was still trying to take care of my teenaged boys and get them to basketball on time. So it was a few months and a few more dizzy spells before I finally got to the doctor.

And it turned out I had a brain tumor. Just a small one.

This should have taken me further into despair, I guess, but actually it did the opposite. I toughened up a bit, kind of slapped myself across the face. The world falling apart, not knowing whether I could trust my own perceptions . . . I couldn't deal with that. But illness? Meh! Illness was doable.

"Okay," I said to the doctor. "What is the next step?"

"Let's find you a neurologist."

I should back up and say that I began my career as a marriage and family therapist before my kids were born, then stepped out to raise them full time when the third son was born. I'd been keeping a toe in the field by occasionally teaching stress management classes for many years. So, the day when I finally got to the neurologist and he told me I'd definitely need to have brain surgery, I knew that the best thing I could do for my body was to laugh. Laughter is an antidote for the toxic effects of stress hormones, and boy, did I have stress hormones! I looked in the newspaper and found a play that sounded funny and dragged one of my teenagers to it. We laughed all evening, which did help.

When we got home at around midnight, the puppy the kids had begged me for needed a walk. "Alf" was a very big black labradoodle with long, skinny legs and a whole bunch of nervous energy. I grabbed the leash and headed out without stopping for a flashlight or a jacket. The puppy was so happy to be out, he pulled frantically at the leash. Several blocks from home, I tripped over a bit of displaced sidewalk and fell flat. I picked myself up and realized I'd broken a finger. It was bleeding and displaced in an ugly way.

I gathered up the dog and headed home. My son, not surprisingly, did not want to go with me to the emergency room. So, I wrapped my hand in a dishtowel and got in the car.

Nature saves us from the serious pain for a while after an injury. I was on the freeway when the grace period was over and huge, throbbing pain erupted in my hand. At the same time, I had a sudden memory of something I'd told my husband in those first couple of weeks after he'd told me he was leaving, that my deepest fear was being old and sick and alone. Well, there I was: old, sick, alone.

It's a miracle that I made it to the hospital. I was weeping so uncontrollably I could barely see the road. I had to sit in the parking lot for a while before I could wipe my eyes on that dishcloth and head inside.

There was no one there. The emergency room was empty. No one at the desk, no one waiting. I stood there, my hand upright, dripping blood on the linoleum because I'd left my dishtowel in the car. Finally someone came out of the locked door, but it was just a visitor, a woman in a tan trench coat, and she was going to the vending machine to get some water. And then she couldn't get back inside either.

We started the kind of awkward conversation people have in the middle of the night in the emergency room: Who are you here with? What happened to your finger? I told her about my dog pulling on the leash and my fall, and she told me that you could buy a collar that made the dog turn instead of pulling. I nodded and told her that I had one of those collars. I just couldn't figure out how to get it on the squirmy dog!

The woman reached into her pocket and brought out her business card. "I own a pet store," she said. "Bring your dog and the collar in. If I'm not there, no worries, one of my employees can help you get the collar on."

I smiled and thanked her. How very kind!

The triage nurse finally arrived at the desk and invited me in. While she was taking my blood pressure and filling out her form, I told her that the broken finger wasn't the worst thing that had happened to me that day. She asked a lot of questions about my tumor and who my surgeon was going to be, then put her hand gently on my forearm.

"Okay, first of all, the kind of tumor you have is almost always benign. And your surgeon is the best in the valley. He's amazing. You are going to be fine."

I started to cry. I didn't know if this was true, but I did know it was such a kind thing to say.

They took me for an x-ray and finally to the doctor, who manipulated the bone into place and put it in a splint, greatly reducing the pain. We started a conversation. It was a very slow night in the emergency room, and we talked for almost an hour. He was a good listener and wanted to know all about my divorce. Another unexpected kindness.

Finally it was time for me to go. They couldn't give me pain meds because I was driving myself home, but they did want to give me a tetanus shot. I sat on a gurney in the middle of the emergency room while I waited.

Suddenly there was a big kerfuffle to which I had a front-row seat. Doctors and nurses appeared out of nowhere, wheeling in an old man in a diabetic coma. I heard that this was the second time he'd been in that night. They got him settled and hooked up to all the machines. And then, as quickly, as they'd appeared, they all disappeared, leaving this man in a coma on the bed in the glass-walled room across from me and his wife in the chair opposite the bed. She was probably in her eighties and obviously exhausted, crumpled in the chair like a discarded toy.

The nurse came and gave me my shot. I was free to go. Any other night, I think I would have left. But I had had so many lessons in kindness that night, I couldn't leave that woman alone in that chair.

I knocked gently on the glass wall near the doorway to the hospital room. The woman looked up.

"I—I'm sorry to bother you," I said. "I saw you sitting here. I brought a book in case I had to wait. It's a very good book. Can I give it to you, to help you pass the time?"

She lit up. It was like when you put a wilted flower in water and it comes to life again.

"Thank you so much!" she said. "I don't need the book. My son will be here soon. I so appreciate the offer, though." Her warm and grateful smile reached all the way through my body, down to my toes.

It was nearly four in the morning when I drove home. I knew that something profound had happened to me that night, and it wasn't just that I had experienced my worst fear . . . and it wasn't that bad. It took me a couple of weeks to process the experience and come to understand the first of the important lessons from the experience.

I'm not alone. None of us are alone. We may be lonely for long stretches. But connection is never far away, even if we can't see it in the moment. The kindness of other people toward me that night was unexpected, undeserved, and very sweet, like the tinkle of sleigh bells. When I was kind to the old woman at the hospital, though, and when my kindness was received with gratitude, that brought a deep and resounding joy, like standing in the belfry and feeling the vibration of the church bell.

Well! I had control over that experience!

I began a mindful diet of kindness exercises. At first, I just decided to take action to be kind to a stranger whenever I was feeling low. This morphed, eventually, into a daily practice. The best part was the fun it was to be on the lookout for opportunities to be kind to strangers. I pulled over into the slow lane, let people in front of me in lines, paid for the coffee of the person behind me at the cash register, scooped up random dog poop on sidewalks, brought newspapers to porches, opened doors for women with strollers . . . and my mood lightened a bit every time. I found that knowing how the other person received my kindnesses actually wasn't important. It was even better to do these kindnesses in secret and imagine making someone's day happier.

As It turned out, the ride to the hospital was the low point of my divorce experience. After that, everything got better. The doctors were able to do a "cyber-knife" laser treatment for my tumor—no surgery! I found my voice in my divorce, and we came to a settlement that was fair for everyone. I restarted my private practice as a marriage and family therapist working with young children and ended up being so successful I decided to expand and hire other therapists to work for me—creating a clinic, the Child & Family Counseling Group, in San Jose, California, that I'm immensely proud of now. And, after a few years of tragicomical serial coffee dating, I found an amazing man to love and to marry.

When the universe leads us to a life-changing moment, it's like a rock thrown into a pond. The ripples that expand outward in waves are large and close together at first, then gradually smooth out and get farther apart. Fourteen years later, I'm still learning what my experience meant in deeper, more profound ways. I'll share just a couple of things I've learned that could be helpful for others.

That night in the hospital was in part about experiencing my worst fear. Enduring it. Feeling every bit of the pain. Diving into the wave instead of running from it. This is not fun. But, on the other side of it is freedom. If you're afraid of heights, find a cliff. Stand on the edge. Endure the vertigo. Welcome it. This will be perhaps the hardest thing you have ever done. Be patient. Wait for it. You may have to do this several times. And then . . . I promise the fear will be gone. Wow. When you can climb mountains without fear, the world is a very big place.

Another tip, I guess, is about the human tendency to fiercely resist change. We know that change is inevitable, but we fight it as if we could prevent earthquakes by reaching into the earth, grabbing hold of those tectonic plates, and holding them together with our bare hands. All of our efforts, though, even if they are successful for a while, fail in the end. The earthquakes happen, perhaps even stronger because our efforts to keep things the same just make the problems worse.

I'd had to work hard to contort my beliefs about my marriage to fit my desperate need for things to stay the same. I had thought, at the time, that my intuition had been wrong, that I couldn't trust it. I've come to understand now, though, that my intuition had been screaming at me for a long time, and I had chosen to stick my fingers in my ears and ignore it.

So. I am human. This is the way all of our brains work, isn't it? Our spiritual practices for tens of thousands of years have tried to tackle this question of how we can circumvent our human tendency to resist and wisely accept the change that is inevitable. And the wisdom the sages have passed on to us is there for the taking, if we only ask. Meditate every day. Pray for guidance. Listen to your intuition even if it is only whispering. Make gratitude, kindness, and compassion a daily, conscious practice.

None of this will prevent earthquakes. Earthquakes are inevitable. People fall out of love. They become ill. They die. Forget about the little desk. Stand on the edge of the cliff, experiencing the pain all of the way. You can endure it. You are free.

Beth Proudfoot

Beth Proudfoot is a licensed marriage & family therapist with over thirty years of experience helping families with young children to grow and thrive. She's the founder and CEO of the Child & Family Counseling Group, a mental health clinic for children in San Jose, California. Although she no longer works with children individually, she still does some parent coaching around positive discipline, especially for parents of preschoolers. A parent educator for many years, she's co-author of *The Magic of Positive Parenting* (Blackstone Audio), and videos of her "Trailblazing Parenting" class can be found on the Classes page of www.childfamilygroup.com.

Currently, Beth's clinical work focusses on helping parents to divorce with respect and dignity. She went through a collaborative divorce herself many years ago and is passionate about this process, which is the very best thing parents can do for their children during this difficult transition. She works as a child specialist and divorce communications coach in collaborative divorces, helps to mediate the parenting plan for people who are going through mediation, and does some coaching in emotional regulation and communication skills for clients who are litigating their divorce.

Beth lives with her second husband in Sonora, California, on an eleven-acre "ranch" with five active streams and arching oak trees. She has three grown children of her own and three stepchildren—and four grandchildren (and counting!).

Email: **beth@childfamilygroup.com** or **beth@bethproudfoot.com**
Phone: (408) 351-1044, ext. 1
Websites: **www.childfamilygroup.com**, **www.bethproudfoot.com**
Facebook pages: **https://www.facebook.com/sanjoseparenting**,
https://www.facebook.com/divorceoptions
LinkedIn: **https://www.linkedin.com/in/beth-proudfoot-82b9835/**

MUSIC IN MY HEAD
BY HOLLY CHADWICK

Can you hear the music in your head? I hear music in my head, and I can't think of a time when it wasn't there. There was a time I refused to listen, and it came crashing through in a time of crisis. Almost twenty years ago, I became a caregiver of my ill grandparents for a period of time. They had raised me from a baby, and I got to care for them for their last years on Earth. I numbed myself doing this work, as I hated to see them in their declining conditions. Weeks after they died, the music in my head came crashing through as an auditory hallucination and jump-started my inner guidance system during a dangerous situation to get me to the safety of a hospital. Sound crazy? It can be, and being in a crazy situation is where we are collectively, as, according to CNN, there is an 891% increase in calls to the mental health crisis hotline, and chaos and death ensues as a result of the 2020 pandemic. We're all in a state of crisis in varying degrees if we admit it or not. A lot of us are numbing from their spiritual nature, like I did. According to Aeriol Ascher, this book's compiler it is her "observation as a healing practitioner that if someone cuts themselves off to their spiritual nature so that they cannot trust or access their own intuition or inner knowingness, they often suffer from anxiety or depression. Likewise suffering unprocessed emotions will always eventually show up in the physical body as some sort of condition of dis-ease." I see the pandemic is the precursor to even greater disease and anguish, but there is hope.

My solution for the 2020 global crisis is not to argue about masks and vaccinations, it is to tap into this spiritual side and make decisions based on your inner guidance system. My solution is to not discount the importance of education, and to learn to discern from a variety of news sources, experts, and doctors. Accurate information is there, but this is not a guide to discernment of information in the normal way. Aeriol Ascher perhaps says it best: "It is only by listening to your own inner voice that you can access a true level of discernment between your thoughts and ideas and energies and those of others. It is here where you can start tapping into your own wisdom and your own truth. Once you have a sense of being connected to your own source energy you can direct your energy in ways that support you, your loved ones and your greater community." That's how we work together to discern the conflicting information: it is by listening to the music in your head that is there. The key is to not be terrified. The music in your head jumpstarts your inner guidance system. Now, it may not be specifically music to you, but it's your soul calling out to listen to guidance from source, God, the Universe, whatever you want to call it. It's there, and we collectively must use this time to turn within and listen. Listening within and finding peace with the sense of self and guidance from source is how we make peace with each other.

Now, I am talking about spirituality that is beyond old-fashioned dogma, beyond the New Age love-and-light brand. I'm talking about our connections on the soul level that make us human and our connection to the planet and universe. Ignoring our connection, identifying the "other" is where our trouble lies. Astrophysicist Neil deGrasse Tyson says that "we are all connected; to each other, biologically. To the earth, chemically. To the rest of the universe, atomically." I'd like to think of spirituality as discovering this connection, and, in the spirit that Morgan Freeman explored what we mean by God in the TV series *The Story of God*, people are sharing their interpretations of this connection, this spirituality, by doing their meditations, doing other spiritual practices, and sharing their experiences in conversation across the globe. Smaller meditation, spiritual, and conversation groups are popping up on Zoom and social media. Forgotten books on philosophy are being read. Bridging differences in philosophy is happening. Westerners are reading Eastern thought and attempting to meld the two poles. Books such as *The Resonance Code* by Spring Cheng dare to bridge Eastern and Western thought, and a massive amount of online study groups are popping up in the face of all the commercials and politicians lulling us to sleep. They want us to simply veg out on too many episodes of *Game of Thrones* and reality TV such as *The Tiger King*. As people wake up from the matrix, people are sick of reality TV. And, as our reality has become too scary, they don't know how to handle the crisis or find ways of outside-the-box thinking to defy logic of the old normal. As the amount of new Hollywood content is dwindling due to the studios being shut down, independent, outside-the-box content is thriving.

As humans, we have developed a lot of tools to help with understanding information and tools to harness the music found inside in meditation practice. I don't have all the answers on actions, but I've lived through the terror and am developing a tool. And for the past several years, I've partnered with a technology company developing artificial intelligence for the health and wellness of humans as a guiding hand for mental health. **It has become my mission to train a virtual mental health assistant with my traumatic experiences, and hopefully the experiences of others, to find new ways to educate and unlock acceptance of what I call hearing music in your head.** For the last three years, I have been working to develop technology to help jumpstart all our inner guidance systems. Because I've shared my story so openly in an award-winning Amazon series and two bestselling books and now a third, I've met a lot of cutting-edge doctors in a variety of wellness fields who recognize this music as well and have out-of-this-world explanations to harness this inner guidance system grounded in science. Just read the rest of the stories in this book, and you will find wisdom from healers here. In this chapter is my story of how I hear music in my head and how I used it jump-start my own inner guidance system.

I had what doctors called an extreme grief reaction to my grandparents' deaths. They were my world, and when they were gone, there was no room for my sort of grief in society. My grief was so extreme, I heard the most beautiful music in the universe. It was a cross between angels' voices with orchestral music played on unknown instruments that reverberated my soul to the point that it terrified me. I was terrified that I had become my mother who couldn't raise me. I was afraid I had inherited her mind. The mind of a schizophrenic. I was hearing music in surround sound without a stereo, and the terror that I was hallucinating drove me to have an uncontrollable urge to splash within the pulsating and crashing waves off the ocean off the island in the middle of the night. I thought the waves would make the music go away. Indeed, it would have if I got within the freezing water. I may I have died.

Terrified, I ran outside, barefoot in my pajamas on a cold January night, and got tripped up on the way to the water's edge by a thicket of cherry trees. Falling into the cold, frosty grass shocked me, and I realized I would not get to the water's edge. Something kicked in during that shock of cold: what I believe was my inner guidance system. I knew that I was in trouble. So I started salsa dancing, made up my own music, contrary to the beat of the music in my head that terrified me. I was barefoot, and all the friendly neighbors' driveways were graveled to make it to their doorstep. I was on my way dancing back to my paved driveway and, on the way, hitched a ride with a confused early-morning newspaper delivery man and literally danced my way to the hospital, where I stayed in a psych ward for a week. He must have thought I was crazy, as I was nonverbal but danced to the music on his car radio in the passenger seat before passing out.

When I came to, I heard angry screams of the delivery man kicking me out of his car as a kind man guided me to the door of a building. I found myself at what I recognized as a drug rehab center, but as soon as they looked into my clear eyes and realized I was not on drugs, I was escorted by a policeman to the psych ward at the nearest hospital. I stayed there a week and met an art therapist there, who I met privately with weekly for a year, who helped my slow crawl back to sanity a reality.

We are at a time now that there still is no room for grief, especially grief like this, in society other than the attitude to take a few days off for the funeral and get on with life. When millions of people are dying from the pandemic and their loved ones remain, there needs to be room for grief. I feel like my experience of having an extreme grief reaction gave me a kind of boot camp for the time at hand. It's important to recognize and give room for grief, no matter the size. People aren't as lucky as me to get the help they need. The imperativeness of addressing this need should be obvious. People are terrified.

And hearing your own music in your head can be terrifying. Why terror? Because we are seeing things for as they are and realizing how much uncertainty and how much power we have. What do we do with that power? I find that this quote from Roshi Joan Halifax, PhD, Buddhist teacher, Zen priest, anthropologist, and pioneer in the field of end-of-life care gives direction: "Wise hope, in my estimation, is not seeing things unrealistically, but seeing things as they are, including the truth of suffering and that suffering can be transformed. This kind of hope comes alive through realizing that we don't know what will happen and that in the spaciousness of uncertainty, it is also the space in which we can act." We are all in the space, and either we listen and act, or go back to sleep.

Since my slow recovery, I've been privileged to seek out circumstances that have led me to become the poster child for mental health for a new educational Health Insurance Portability and Accountability Act (HIPAA) compliant platform to deliver wisdom from cutting-edge providers for their patients. This technology is already being used in hospitals such as the Mayo Clinic and Barnes Healthcare for heart disease, diabetes, and autism. The last two years have kicked my ambitions in overdrive, and I now know why I had what I call my bootcamp twenty years ago, and what my purpose here on the planet is. I am licensing this technology to create something I call StoryGuide, specifically to use the technology for mental health in a post-pandemic world.

On StoryGuide, Rubi, the mental health virtual assistant, helps match your personal story to the best provider programs. It could be meditations, a piece of education, a course, a book, or a way to sign up for coaching if you resonate with a particular provider. Rubi is named after my boat, *Rubicon*. The word means "the point of no return." And for a year, I lived on my boat, training Rubi to respond to situations such as mine while networking with cutting-edge professionals.

One professional I met was psychotherapist and humanitarian Jennifer van Wyck, who currently is in a posting with the Red Cross to help with the COVID crisis in the Philippines. She published a book a year ago called *The Good Thing About Mortar Shells: Choosing Love Over Fear*, and this book—and her meditations and courses that go along with the book—are to be featured in StoryGuide. Through this education and firsthand experiences of someone who has visited war-torn countries to help people out of the aftermath, you can learn how to choose love over fear.

I met cutting-edge professionals such as Dr. Beth Halbert, also featured in this book. Her "inner family" modality shifted my perspective of the story I tell myself that identifies myself and shapes reality. I've learned to be aware of this story and all the roles my inner-family play in this story to make sure this story is serving me best. I hope you refer to her chapter in this book to learn more. On StoryGuide, you too can learn how to tell yourself the best story that suits all aspects of yourself and serves as an inner guidance system to set you up for success.

Currently, I am still doing pilots with doctors for StoryGuide, as we have new features to have Rubi integrate with Zoom and wearables that are sleep trackers such as Whoop. Check out more about StoryGuide at www.StoryGuide.ai and feel free to join the mailing list. If you're a practitioner that wants to participate, please let me know! I have a memoir coming out soon and will be launching the product after a seed round of funding in 2022.

The pandemic is a great reset, a pause from our normal to turn within and listen to our inner guidance system to make steps to the new normal. May the music in our head let us find the steps as a dance. Be playful; learn to choose love over fear. Our story doesn't have to be a tragedy. We can learn to choose the next chapter together.

Holly Chadwick

Holly Chadwick was raised on Whidbey Island by her grandparents, who believed in rigorous music studies to combat the trauma of coming from parents that had mental illness. Though she didn't become a concert pianist, she has directed short movies, documentaries, and now a web series called *Sounds of Freedom*. She earned a BA in Film and Digital Media from the University of California, Santa Cruz and has studied fine art and digital media as far away as Italy and The Banff Centre in Alberta, Canada.

At the age of sixteen, Holly was a key member in a successful Internet start-up and went on to working for fine art and newspaper publishing companies in design and advertising, as well as in a darkroom developing crime scene photos.

Holly's father, who suffered with post-traumatic stress disorder, was the inspiration for *Sounds of Freedom*. She is also working on a documentary featuring her mother, mental illness, and herself called *Music in My Head*, based on her memoir coming out in 2022 of the same name.

Holly has recently found herself living in a log cabin in the southern United States (northern Georgia). She lives with her husband and two large dogs and enjoys kayaking, sailboating, playing piano, photography, and off-roading adventures.

Sign up for info about Holly's latest book coming out here: www.storyguide.org/musicinmyhead/

And you can follow her projects at the following links:

Websites: **www.storyguide.ai**,
eideticfilm.com, soundsoffreedomtheseries.com
Facebook:
facebook.com/storyguideAI
facebook.com/soundsoffreedomtheseries
Other social media:
twitter.com/storyguideAI
twitter.com/holly_chadwick
instagram.com/storyguide.ai
instagram.com/soundsoffreedomtheseries
TikTok: **@StoryGuide.ai**

FINDING PEACE PROFOUND
BY AERIOL ASCHER

I remember it like it was some magical dream: the moment I settled into my divine purpose. Honestly, I had felt it before; I had even been living it out loud in my life—my business, my creative projects, and my teaching. I have to tell you this was at such a vast and deep level, with such synchronicity, it was as if it were orchestrated by the divine.

I will tell you about the important pieces of this story, but I will also tell you that the beginning of my story actually starts many years ago and is connected to my soul's mystical roots in other lifetimes, if your consciousness is open to that level or interpretation.

This part of my own personal story—the part that I am submitting for this beautiful anthology, *Awakened Leaders: Empowering Stories of Self-Healing, Triumph and Transformation*—starts in 2021. Although I had had amazing success early in the year with my book *Empowered Self-Care: Healing Body, Mind, and Soul for a Better World*, I had also experienced a dramatic tidal wave of loss, grief, and traumatic stress when, in quick succession, I lost a longtime friend, I lost my cat, one of my dogs had a spinal injury and lived, another dog had a spinal injury and died, and a friend from my neighborhood was killed just a block from our home on his motorcycle.

I had been speaking about self-care and really taking my own self-care practice from a body mind soul perspective very seriously for several years and felt that I had reached a respectable level of consistency with myself. Thank goodness. I absolutely would not have survived the shutdown and radical shift of 2020 if it had not been for my dedication to radical self-care and being committed and congruent with my own self-healing and self-mastery practice.

It was summertime, and I reached out to an old friend to catch up and connect after the long eighteen-month shut-in that prevented us from gathering and pretty much killed my whole social life altogether. We had decided to meet for coffee and take a walk at the labyrinth located at Rosicrucian Egyptian Park in San Jose, California. This particular friend and I had connected for years over our mutual interest in spiritual and paranormal subjects, so he had been agreeable to walk the labyrinth and set forth some intentions to create magic in our lives. We had no idea how quickly my intentions would be met, and it only became evident in the retelling of the story how instantaneously the universe can shift to reveal its everyday magic.

"Have you ever thought of being involved with the Rosicrucians?" my friend casually inquired.

Just then, we saw a large door to our right open and a tall, skinny gentleman hidden behind some oversized glasses peek his head out and prop open the tall door that I now know to be the entrance to the temple. As if divinely timed for our benefit, he looked our way and spoke to us: "Are you here to join us for our Council of Solace meditation?"

Never being one to pass up an invitation to the divine, I was an insta-yes! We were invited to enter the temple. What a thrilling turn our coffee date had taken as we entered the temple door and stepped reverently into a dark atrium with a beautiful photo portrait from under the head of the Sphinx from Egypt dimly lit and illuminating a wonderful space with a palpable presence that soaked deeply into my being. I found a socially distanced space across from the illuminated Sphinx and settled myself in silent meditation as directed by our host. As I focused on my breathing and allowed myself to be present in the anticipation, I waited for things to begin.

"What a cool space," my monkey brain chatted, and I surveyed the area. "I could get into coming to this beautiful environment to do group mediation like this . . ." I exhale, two, three, four. "Oh my goodness, this is awesome!"

Letting my breath go, two, three, four. "When will it start?" Holding my breath... "Remember to breathe! Pay attention," two, three, four.

As I mentally danced with the voice in my head and settled deeply into my body, our host closes the temple door and walks into the atrium, crisply turning at the corners of his trail, leaving his path both intentional and clean. He approaches a gong precariously placed in the corner of what I thought was our meditation space, and I gleefully awaited the resonance that I anticipated for an instrument of that size and weight. Sure enough, he struck the gong, sending a sound energy wave that I could viscerally feel permeate my body and psychically witness traverse through the entire space, clearing a still and sacred container in its powerful wake. I reverently relished the moment and realized that was only just the introduction to what was a homecoming to my heart in the moments to come.

"Those wishing to join our meditation may do so by presenting themselves at the temple door," our host announced in a deeply resonant and formal tone, and he opened up yet another door, this one being the actual temple.

"Oh my gosh! There is more?!" My inner self leapt through my chest as I watched a few of the experienced guests file through the tall door as our host stood calmly at attention next to the open portal.

When it was my turn to enter the temple, I felt a very strong sense of coming home and of vastness, stillness. It was hard to take in the simple and elegant beauty that instantly transported me to somewhere ancient in my soul. The raised ceiling was dimly lit and gave the distinct impression of the celestial night sky.

Both sides of the space were lined with benches. I had felt like this before. I had seen this before. I had a distinct memory of a meditation I attended in Mount Shasta, California, at a Wesak festival at a local city college when, while enjoying the presentation of a local monk, suddenly I had this impression of the people in the bleachers around me being light beings that I had traveled with for eternity. I know it sounds weird, but it was extremely engrained in my memory and invoked by the monk and his whimsical sharing and audience participation of singing the Beatles song "All You Need Is Love." I digress, but only for a moment.

As I take in the stately columns and beautiful Egyptian scenes of initiation that fill the room and the walls of the sacred space, I breathe in the succulent scents of incense and allow myself to be transported. I perch on a bench in the back of the space and wait for our host to secure the portal of the sacred space and begin his angular journey towards the podium near the front of the space.

As his deep and resonant voice guides us, I am transported from my body far above the Earth. He directs us to hold the entire Earth in our mind's eye and send it loving and pure energy. "No problem, I have a picture just like this as my screensaver on my phone," I ponder. "Shhhhhh! Pay attention. There is something for you here," the voice in my head gently reminds me as I exhale, two, three, four.

We are taken on a journey, sending our healing intentions and love to individuals, to humanity, to specific areas of the world, and finally we were asked to turn our intention deeply inward and to allow the grace and energies to fill *us* up. It was time for us to receive. I opened my heart and masterfully emptied my monkey mind for a brief moment.

"Let us now intone the vowel Om." The booming voice woke me from my stillness.

"OM," the small group timidly sounded in the open and resonant space.

"OM," the voices stronger and more confident this time. I savored the overtones and variances I heard as my fellow souls made their voices ring in the sacred chamber.

"OM," adding a harmonic top note to the symphony of souls. I felt my eyes well up and my heart swell.

"By Cosmic Law, So Mote It Be!" our host declared, his voice cutting through the palpable silence with intention and authority.

And just like that, the atrium door swung open, the gong was struck, and it dissipated through the space and through my body as if solidifying the intentions that the group put forward both personally and collectively. We were directed by our host to exit the temple. This is my work. The work of a mystic. This alchemical moment was so real and so true to me in that there was nowhere I could hide from myself.

Through the dark atrium I made my way to the almost blinding light outside. Even this symbolic act evoked so much illumination and knowing inside of me, I almost felt that my physical body could not contain it. I felt as if I was occupying many lifetimes at once, overlaid upon each other, and as I exited the temple past the columns that guarded the entry, I let the sunlight warm my body and the light cut away the blurry jet lag fogging my consciousness as I returned from my mystical journey traversing through time and space. Delicious.

"What did you think?" My friend who I came with tapped me on the shoulder to wake me from my reverie.

"I'm hooked," I affirmed. Just then, our host appeared with a periodical. He handed it to me and thanked me for coming. I noticed that it featured a few articles on meditation and self-healing. I graciously received the volume and flipped through the pages in disbelief at the similarity and synchronicity with the work I was bringing forward in my own books and teachings. How was this even possible?

I knew in that moment I was home. This is exactly where I was supposed to be. There was so much for me here. I could learn, meditate, and be in community with like-minded individuals who had no other agenda than to assist in raising the consciousness of the planet and empowering individuals with divine knowledge of the self.

In the following days and weeks, I joined the Rosicrucian Order and began going to the Council of Solace meditation at the San Jose Rosicrucian Temple at least once a week. It was so affirming for me to add this ritual into my weekly lifestyle and daily routine, and I took this commitment to my *self* very seriously. Please do understand that, oftentimes, my inner-*self* cut the timing close, and I found myself hustling up to the temple doors at 11:59 a.m. for the 12:00 p.m. meditation!

I need to take a moment to explain here: time is a great equalizer that we as humans must respect. It is a group agreement that we must all keep as a sign of respect for others and a matter of consciousness for yourself. Besides—and I think this is a profound statement for so many reasons—*if you miss the opening of the portal, you will not make it through to the inner atrium and ultimately into the temple itself before the ceremony begins and the container of the sacred space is sealed.* You would literally miss the boat. So I put this new, upgraded spiritual commitment of mine to the test by making a physical commitment of time and energy to make it to the ceremony live and in person on a weekly basis.

I am only a new student and initiate of the Rosicrucian Order; however, I have been a student of metaphysics and the divine, on my own self-healing journey, and professionally assisting others to embark on their own self-mastery quest for three decades. There are many ways to connect to your divine essence and to uncover your soul purpose.

I'm excited to continue to teach and to support others to connect with their soul purpose. The *Self-Mastery Journal: Awakening Divine Purpose* will support you in taking the journey to a deeper level for you. It can be found on Amazon or at my website: www.AeriolAscher.com.

I also recommend to any of my clients, friends, or anyone whom I may encounter that if you become interested in the Rosicrucian Order you can look them up online at Rosicrucian.org and see for yourself if you happen to resonate with their mystical and philosophical teachings about awakening the divine self within. The Council of Solace meditation is done Monday through Friday at noon at the Rosicrucian Temple in San Jose, California, on behalf of all those souls who need assistance or healing. Perhaps I will someday see you there.

I hope that you will find your own divine connection and a spiritual community to support you in your mystical and self-healing pursuits. I am available for life purpose readings, guidance, and self-care support at my website. Remember also that I offer publishing and multimedia visibility programs for holistic practitioners, transformational coaches, and spiritual teachers to support the voices of healing to evolve consciousness on the planet via AskAeriol Coaching, Aeriol Publishing, and the BodyMindSoul.TV & Media Network.

I hope you have read my story and you have started to feel an opening to discover your peace and some patterns or habits you can build into your life to support you on a regular basis.

Most of all, may you find Peace Profound.

Aeriol Ascher

Aeriol Ascher MsD is a #1 international best-selling author many times over. She is a holistic educator, an empowerment leader, and voice and presence coach from San Jose, California. She is the founder, producer, and host of the *Positive Vibes with Aeriol: Healing Body Mind and Soul* podcast and VoiceAmerica.TV show and the proud recipient of three Communicator Awards of Distinction from the Academy of Interactive Visual Arts.

Aeriol's recent book compilation *Empowered Self-Care: Healing Body, Mind, and Soul for a Better World* became a bestseller in fifty-six categories across five countries, and twenty-one of those categories made it to the #1 position. It is Aeriol's personal mission to raise the consciousness of the planet one soul at a time, and she believes that by leading, producing, and publishing holistic media and programs that educate, uplift and inspire self-mastery, she is doing her part.

As a holistic educator, Aeriol empowers her clients with tools to increase body awareness, hone intuition, and give voice to their highest self so they can confidently and authentically navigate their personal and professional lives. As a book compiler and empowerment leader, she has a passion for guiding heart-centered entrepreneurs, practitioners, educators, and coaches to show up, speak up, and stand out so they can embrace their authentic and soul-aligned success.

Whether you are a leader in need of self-care support or you are on a full-blown mission to get your voice heard and your passion published—or both—you will want to lean in and join the BodyMindSoul.TV & Media Network.

https://www.facebook.com/Acriol
https://www.facebook.com/AskAeriol
https://www.facebook.com/reikiangelacademy
https://www.instagram.com/askaeriol/
https://youtube.com/c/HealingBodyMindandSoulNetwork
https://www.linkedin.com/in/aeriolascher/

PART TWO

BUILDING A LEGACY

"What counts in life is not the mere fact that we have lived. It is what difference we have made to the lives of others that will determine the significance of the life we lead."
—Nelson Mandela

ONE DECISION CAN CHANGE YOUR LIFE
BY APRIL SHOEMAKER

One momentous day that altered the rest of my life happened when I got mad at my mother and the world. In that moment, with the steely will of an eight-year-old, I quit on life. I quit trying to win my mother's games or to make her happy; I quit trying to find and speak my truth; and I decided to adapt and endure until life was over. Then I forgot that I made that decision, and it ran like a brilliantly designed software program in the background of my life until I rediscovered it as an adult. My automatic behavior became adapting and enduring the situations that showed up. It never occurred to me that I could/should stand up for myself and find out who I was or how to follow my heart, even after I moved away from my crazy, terrifying mother. My strengths involved fading into the background, reading the people around me so I could take care of their needs before they knew they had a need, and reading situations for danger while keeping myself safe, quiet, and in the background.

The year before, when I was seven and thought I knew everything about life, I was desperately seeking my spiritual community. Part of the reason I gave up at eight is that by that time I *knew* my spiritual community did not exist. After moving to my third house, attending two grade schools, and checking out our church, I knew I was all alone and had been abandoned by God.

Forgetting my decision to give up on life and to adapt and endure until life was over, I spent a lifetime trying to figure out my screwy family and why I didn't feel I belonged anywhere. I was reading all the books I could find on self-help and family therapy. I got my BA in psychology and an MA in guidance and counseling, attempting to heal and understand myself. I studied every form of therapy I could find and became trained in most of them, trying to fix what felt like my inherently flawed self but was really my wounded inner child. Even after I discovered the eight-year-old's decision, it took years to undo the damage of my ingrained and automatic behaviors.

At thirty-three, I prayed that all my inner work had healed my emotional wounds when I discovered I was pregnant. Immediately I started looking for ways to set my child up for being true to himself, to follow his inner voice, to be self-confident, self-reliant, happy, and to know that he's loved unconditionally . . . all things I did not have for myself. I followed my inner guidance each step along the way, glad that I was alone and didn't have to explain my wild ideas to someone else so that I could just do what I thought was best for my child, starting with orchestrating an underwater birth.

I gave birth to my son at home, in a cattle trough following the guidelines in a book by a couple in Texas, after my favorite rebirthing author, Sondra Ray, described the process as the most peaceful method of childbirth, in *Ideal Birth*. I then found an experienced midwife to support me in conducting my wild plan for a home birth. Anyone who asked, "Aren't you afraid the baby will drown?" was not invited to the birth, which was all of my co-workers and family members. I also came from the premise that I didn't know how to raise a child for a future I can't predict, as technology is moving so fast. I knew I needed new ways of thinking, acting, and certainly parenting. I did this by staying in state of curiosity and by getting present to my son as a person, asking myself, "What would empower him?" and following my inner guidance. I treated him like a person, with respect and trust, as I taught him how to do things I knew how to do, encouraging him to think and act independently in age-appropriate ways as well as make executive decisions for himself: not just letting him choose between two things I've already chosen, but letting him make decision about his activities, such as which friend's house he was going to, etc., without consulting me first. I was able to provide him with a powerful sense of self despite my own lack of self-confidence and wounded soul.

In 2000, I took the Landmark Forum and added new levels of transformation to my life and was able to teach Jason how to be production supervisor of his own life at age thirteen, and I taught him how to make unreasonable requests of adults (in a very respectful way) and have his life work despite my flaws and shortcomings.

In 2006, when I moved from Michigan to California to go on staff at the headquarters of Landmark Worldwide, Jason was a sophomore at University of Michigan, and I was looking for something we could do when he visited. We started to play Kiosyki's *Cash Flow* game, which teaches people how to manage money so that they can get out of the rat race by creating passive income and stop trading hours for dollars. Even though I read the books, took Kiosyki's seminars, and played the game, my son actually put it into action and bought a three-bedroom house when he graduated from college, renting the extra rooms out to cover the mortgage, starting his voyage into real estate investing, which he continues to do ten years later, on his way to getting out of the rat race while in his thirties.

At twenty-three, Jason asked me to write a parenting book about how I empowered him differently than other parents. I thought it was funny because he didn't even know I was asking myself that question! We wrote *Empowering Parenting* together as a project even though we were 2,400 miles apart. At the time, I was untrained and unprepared to do all the social media tasks he recommended, not to mention wondering *who was I* to write about parenting (?!). Thus the Kindle books just sat neglected on Amazon until they disappeared.

Years later, all that I put into parenting a great human being was returned to me tenfold. I was struggling financially after losing my job, and, using his skill as a business consultant, Jason looked for ways he could empower me rather than continue to rescue me financially. He called it Operation Mom, sending me an email with freelance suggestions to use my writing, editing, caretaking skills, and more. He introduced me to Uber and Lyft, and although I wasn't sure it was for me, I have been happily driving for them since 2014.

I always told people that I parented like a gymnast spotter, letting my son try out new things on his own while being there to catch him if he stumbled or fell. He did that for me as he flew in on a Sunday, helped me with each step to buy a new car, including financing it with a low interest rate with his good credit, and letting me pay him each month for the car. He had already put things into motion to sell my current car, which was too old to use for Uber, helped me finish details to start driving with Uber, and get the best deal on insurance. I saw all the ways I would have quit on myself and would have failed if he hadn't been there to ensure I followed through with everything. For someone who is used to being a lone ranger, I resisted needing a gymnast-spotter, but he supported me in engaging in new behaviors and following through to completion. Surprisingly, I was driving by Thursday of that week and had $1,000 in my pocket after the sale of my old car. It rocked my world with what's possible and has allowed me to thrive financially beyond any of my earlier jobs.

I am brilliant in things my son is not: listening on a deep level, hearing younger conversations running the show, knowing where the deep wounds are, and hearing misconceptions people have about themselves. I can tell people about aspects of their astrology chart, how to improve their life with *feng shui*, or glean information from a number of different therapeutic processes I'm trained in. I often empower my Uber/Lyft customers as they are trying to calm down before they go on a job interview or are overwhelmed by life because they don't know that they are an empath, or I make them laugh with all my parenting stories.

However, the financial world where my son is highly skilled, has a passion for, and is invested in being successful. I have such a low interest and emotional connection to that world that it's hard for me to put in the necessary work to do more than the minimum. Of course, I occasionally feel like a failure about finances when I feel that I "should" be further along, but not enough to work on it. I can now see that it was the damaged view of myself that kept me struggling and unable to see or become what I was capable of.

My son's next intervention caught me by surprise as he wanted to know what my credit score was so he could help me buy a fourplex, live in one of the units, and rent the others out. Operation Mom struck again. Years ago, he told me to establish credit because I was running on a cash basis. Then, of course, since my self-sabotage was still high, I maxed out my credit and kept it that way for the next few years, spending money to build a business yet not taking appropriate actions.

When he approached me, I had to keep looking at the bigger picture as I felt like a failure again. I could see how I was being lazy and only making enough to get by and letting my credit card debt accumulate needlessly. By this time, I had healed my wounded inner child but never figured out how to work successfully in the world until my son held my hand and guided me out of the darkness again, with no judgment, just love and logic.

I don't know what was more embarrassing, revealing my $4,000 in credit card debt or sharing the passwords for my accounts so he could pay my cards off—created in moments of frustration, like yesyousuck888.

The process just blew my mind and woke me up. I had gone from $0 credit in 2013 to $8,000 credit by 2017. That was more than I ever had, and I didn't think about it further. When he came and paid off my credit card debt, giving me a loan at 4% rather than the 24% I was paying for my credit cards, my credit score went from 630 (fair) to 764 (excellent). Over the next year the amount of credit grew to $20,200, and I learned how to responsibly manage my credit cards and make money doing it. This process really woke me up to new levels of playing with money, which has been really jarring to my self-image and sense of self-worth!

What was overwhelming for me about being successful in the world was matter-of-fact for him and made smart business sense. I realized I needed to quit beating myself up for not being that way, and honor and respect my ways and his without judging his to be better than mine. They are simply different.

I realized that I had to stop trusting my emotional view of myself and acknowledge what I've accomplished and contributed. I know that people see me as a strong, solid, powerful, loving person who has made a difference in their lives when I look beyond my emotional assessment.

In terms of healing my eight-year-old's program of adapting and enduring, I had to use all my tools and processes. My main tactic was to get present to the rules of the existing program: no games, or throwing my heart into the mix, stay invisible and quiet, settle for scraps, and use makeshift solutions to survive. **I then authored what I wanted in life: to create and thrive.** This included creating lots of games and adventures; throwing my whole self into life; being bold, brave, and visible; to find and express my authentic self; create a great lifestyle; and build quality structures, patterns, and habits. No more makeshift! I looked at what emotions I wanted to experience in life, and I chose fulfillment, satisfaction, engagement, flow, and inspiration. Instead of focusing on my complaints about life, I began to be sourced by happiness regardless of my circumstances.

In summary, we try hard to do the right things to lead, when sometimes it's a decision in the moment that changes the direction of our lives and inadvertently empowers another.

If I had been a workaholic like my son, I wouldn't have quit my high-level technical writing job, working forty-plus hours a week. The childcare staff would have raised him instead of me. However, I decided to stay at home and raise him in my unique ways and forget that I was ever a high-level professional in my sweet size-10 business suits.

If I hadn't asked the roofer working on my house to teach my nine-year-old son how to walk on the roof safely, Jason probably wouldn't have kicked off his snowboard in his twenties to rescue a young girl caught in the tow ropes by jumping on the roof to help the attendant free her hand and get her down.

If I hadn't been trying to improve my financial acumen, I wouldn't have spent my hard-earned money to attend Robert Kiosyki seminars and buy the *Cash Flow* Game. And, if I hadn't taken a job a five-hour flight away from my son, we wouldn't have played the game for hours on end during every visit, which trained my son to manage his finances at an elevated level.

If I hadn't empowered my son to follow his inner guidance and follow his own path by respecting him as a person, giving him the right to make executive decisions for himself at a young age, he probably wouldn't have come back to create Operation Mom in such a way that he empowered me when I got lost, and gave me the tools to win, twice.

Start where you are, follow your heart, and be your unique brand of leadership. Stop beating yourself up. Stop being a lone ranger, and pair up with someone who has the skills you need. Take in the compliments and honor your superpowers.

All this is to say, you don't need to take giant steps to make a big splash. Start where you are, and take small steps in ways that empower yourself and others. You might be surprised how life turns out!

April Shoemaker

April Shoemaker, inspired by her son's request, wrote *Empowering Parenting* e-books, providing abundant resources and stories. Using her witty sense of humor, she naturally sparks new ways of thinking that make a difference for others. Attending the Conference for Global Transformation, April created a poster on the *Lessons of Workability from Villains*, inspiring people to tap their inner villain. At the event she asked people: "Are you out creating like a villain (minus the evil nature) or waiting for problems to fix like a superhero?" The next year, April won an Editor's Choice award for her paper on "Parenting as an Inquiry" (2016), sharing her parenting journey as a vehicle to introduce a powerful strategy to relate to the person/situation in front of you in the present, rather than from a bundle of reactions loaded with past-based emotions.

April is a highly trained life coach with a proven track record of helping people create their lives newly, using variety of processes including healing inner child, rebirthing, family therapy, NLP, distinctions from Landmark Worldwide training, and more. She has a master's in guidance and counseling and is currently diving deep into her inner child issues, searching for ways to help others not be stuck in the past by their childhood fears, decisions, and adaptive behaviors. April loves assisting people in reinventing themselves. She is committed to everyone being healthy, loving, joyful, and creative. She is also currently working on earning her PhD in metaphysics.

lovelaughempower@gmail.com
1-510-355-4668
https://www.facebook.com/april.shoemaker1
https://www.facebook.com/lovelaughempower
https://www.linkedin.com/in/aprilshoemaker/
https://twitter.com/April56053255
https://www.youtube.com/c/AprilShoemaker26

THE TRANSFORMATIVE POWER OF FAMILY
BY DIANA POHLE, PHD

My transformation story is about a season in my life full of abundant blessings that unfolded because of what I attribute to divine intervention and open hearts. It is a personal journey that makes perfect sense in hindsight but was anything but as I muddled my way through it. It is a story of personal healing and learning to lead through love, detachment, and trust. It is my hope that this story may be a growth catalyst for you on your own transformational journey.

Trusting the Divine

A divorced mother of two and long since remarried, I sat watching the news one evening while reeling from another gut-wrenching loss of a child through miscarriage. Then a serendipitous news story ignited a chain of events that has since changed my world. The story that caught my attention was that of the plight of orphaned children following the conflict in Syria. Immediately, I thought about those mothers who wanted their children safe and yet were taken violently from this world and no longer physically able to protect them. I thought of the little ones I conceived yet was never able to hold that I could only hope were enveloped by love in the heavens. I was overwhelmed with the strongest conviction that if I could not raise those babies, I could be the heart and hands for one of those mamas. Thankfully, my husband's heart was equally as receptive to my divinely inspired idea, and together we naively embarked on the most rewarding journey of growing our family through less-conventional means.

In 2014 and through a series of events that can only be poorly explained without attribution to a higher power, we welcomed our third, and then our fourth, and then our fifth child. Over a few more years, our household would grow, one by one, to a home full of nine amazing young people. Seven of our children originated from a small country in East Africa and came to us as unaccompanied refugee minors, termed URMs by the Office of Refugee Resettlement. My life was profoundly and forever changed by my children, incredible souls I have the privilege of journeying this life alongside of, and the many lessons they have taught me along the way.

No Longer Glorifying "The Doing"

We all come with baggage. I am certainly no exception. Despite unsolicited words of wisdom that well-meaning individuals frequently tried to bestow upon me since my youth—"you care too much" or "you wear your heart on your sleeve"—for as long as I can remember, I have always seen the world as an unfair place where vulnerable people needed protecting. I could not comprehend how many people filter out others' suffering and rationalized that I must be able to sacrifice a little more than some others to make things better for the people, or causes, that concerned me. Paired with a high need for achievement, this misplaced martyrdom, along with ability, led me to pursue achievements and roles where I felt I could make a difference for the greater good. I felt a strong sense of obligation and responsibility to take on leadership roles at work and in church bodies, community organizations, and not-for-profit organizations with whom I was aligned. If I was involved in a program or activity and saw an opportunity for something to be done better, I instinctively would raise my hand to lead it even if I did so at the expense of my joy, health, or peace. Yet, in time and through a beautiful gift of family, I came to understand that in my glorification of "the doing," I was not really leading at all. It was about me and feeling that I needed to accumulate accomplishments in order to be of value. This insight was one of the most fundamental changes that started it all. One thing was for certain, as a parent of nine, I needed to seriously evaluate why I was glorifying being busy at the peril of myself and those relationships I valued most. My transformational journey has led me to a new understanding that genuine leadership in our families, in our work, and in the world around us is not about the doing but about authentically leading through love.

Assuming Positive Intent

On the day our family first grew, a social worker dropped our new son at the house with nothing but a bag full of his few belongings immediately following his school day. After an hour of awkwardly staring at each other with little ability to communicate due to a significant language barrier, my anxiety of the silence pushed me to get us out of the house. We went to play miniature golf, we got something to eat, and then we spent the rest of the afternoon at the library. As I sat at a table, my son emerged from the aisles carrying a book in his hands. He placed it next to me on the table and gently nudged it towards me. Though the story bears no resemblance to ours, the title said it all: *The Lost Boy: A Foster Child's Search for the Love of a Family*. In the days that followed, I learned to grow comfortable with the silence and the other ways we could communicate. When we finally had a meeting with an interpreter, I had carefully planned what I wanted to say. The most important message was, "If you choose to be in this family, you are our son, same as our other children. If something seems wrong or is not working for you, please assume positive intent as it is likely a misunderstanding, and we can figure it out together." It is possible I attribute too much to this early discussion, but I do believe assuming positive intent in healthy relationships is a best practice. When you make space for trust at home, at work, or in the community, it is easier to communicate and resolve challenges when they come up.

Appreciating Differences

In the months following our new additions, the preconceived notions of ill-informed individuals around us were becoming increasingly obvious. Although it is a natural human tendency to hold unconscious beliefs that stem from our tendency to organize the outside world from our point of view, challenging our unconscious biases and appreciating differences is key to being an awakened leader. As my family grew, we also grew in religions, culture, and language. The Pohle household quickly shifted to embrace the values, traditions, and culture of our newest additions. Yet, it was difficult for our circle to adapt as quickly as the rest of us. The boys would give their culturally appropriate limp handshakes only to be met with well-intended but misplaced critiques of the importance of a firm handshake. Their lack of eye contact would garner scrutiny despite being a signal of respect and deference to elders in their culture. Eating family style with our hands became a welcomed routine in our home, but eyes would roll when we would dine outside the home and one of the children would forgo tableware for his more familiar eating method. We celebrate real birthdays and "American" birthdays. We celebrate Orthodox, Catholic, and Muslim holy days in our home. Our music, cuisine, dress is a blend of all our collective interests, values, and priorities. If it is important to one of us, it is important to all of us. As in families, leading at work or other capacities is not about developing someone into another version of yourself. Rather, it is about genuinely respecting the values and priorities of those around you and appreciating the uniqueness of each person.

Coaching, Not Controlling

Acknowledging that I did not really learn how to love fully until the time my family grew so profoundly is difficult to admit. However, it is my truth. Not that I was a bad parent, but with the benefit of hindsight, I recognize that I took my relationship with my first two children for granted in some respects. I was their mother, and I thought that afforded me some inherent honor and authority, I suppose. In contrast, receiving the gift of teenagers who were separated from amazing biological families on the other side of the world due to terrible circumstances in an unfair world, my role over time in their lives had potential to become less clear—or, worse, less relevant. My role in my children's lives can sometimes be a vulnerable place to be. This was especially the case in the early years, when some of my children were technically in foster care. Often, well-intentioned but imprudent social workers would propose possible alternate living arrangements to earn good graces with the children, even if it would be to a child's long-term detriment. Let's face it, whether we have raised teenagers or not, we all know that that age is full of a little self-centeredness and drama in even the best of circumstances. Hence, subsidized living with friends or boyfriends/girlfriends can be appealing options to young people for the false sense of freedom it conveys. The fact of the matter is that we all made a choice to be a family. Although

I knew, even years ago, that we were a strong family unit, it felt like the integrity of my family was under constant threat by these social workers during those first few years. It would have been devastating had anyone ever chose to walk away.

Building our family through less-conventional means gave me pause to rethink my relationship with my first two children as well. Of course, there is a natural and necessary imbalance of power when you are raising a small child. You cannot have a rational conversation with a tantruming toddler in the checkout line at the grocery store when they're due for a nap. But, as we evaluate our dynamic relationships with older children, they need room to grow and learn at their own pace. Hierarchy, tradition, and obligation are insufficient pillars to build a meaningful lifelong relationship on. The same holds true for any relationship in our adult lives. We ought to coach, not control.

Concluding Thoughts

I am a humble beneficiary of many awakened leaders, spiritual directors, and talented authors who continue to accompany me along my growth journey. Through our personal quests for truth, as we seek to transform ourselves, we may find that an insight at the right time can strike us in a way that ignites the next round of growth in us. Some ideas I desperately needed for my growth were so challenging to accept initially that I fought them voraciously until inspiration (or resignation) helped me come to a new understanding and ultimate acceptance of what now seems should have been easy to comprehend from the start.

Listed below, please find my tips to help you learn to lead through love:

1. Ask yourself sincerely what you are being nudged to do, and, after proper discernment, trust your intuition and proceed without hesitation.

2. Assess the alignment between how you spend your time and your values. Then, set effective boundaries to protect your priorities so you can stay focused on who and what is most important.

3. Be more intentional. Identify the origin of any impulsive reactions by seeking to understand the actions of others before responding.

Be willing to critically examine your attitudes toward people who are different, recognize your biases, and celebrate the unique gifts of each person in your circle (whether at home, work, or in the community)

4. Give support and guidance rather than dictating instructions and rules.

The catalyst for my transformation to a more awakened leader was about trusting in a divine plan and letting go of control to lead from an authentic place of love. I hope in sharing my story, you are encouraged to explore if taking steps to lead through love brings about the change you want in your homes, your work, or this world.

Diana Pohle

Diana Pohle is a psychologist and healthcare business leader with a reputation for collaborative leadership across organizational boundaries and an ability to build partnerships while drawing out the gifts of people and teams to unite collective talents.

Her North Star is connecting the heart of what drives people with the data that provokes meaningful action to make the world a better place. She leverages extensive analytical skills and a relentless curiosity to produce deep insights, improve decision-making, and guide strategies with unwavering equanimity.

Presently, Diana is the senior director of commercial analytics and insights at a West Coast–based biopharma company that seeks to transform men's and women's health. She has over twenty years of experience in healthcare market intelligence, serves on many philanthropic and industry association boards, and teaches undergraduate courses in business strategy, market research, statistics, and healthcare consumer trends. However, she believes her most important leadership role is within the walls of her own home.

Diana is privileged to be the mother of nine amazing young people. As her family grew through unconventional means, she has become an outspoken advocate for the needs of the vulnerable, including immigrants, foster youth, and unaccompanied refugee minors. She relishes opportunities to share her family experience with kindred spirits who may be contemplating the same path to expanding their own families or desire to change the broken systems that fail too many of our neighbors in need, especially children.

diana@leadingthroughlove.com
http://leadingthroughlove.com/
https://www.facebook.com/TheChangeYouWishToSee

THE ART OF RELATIONSHIP
BY LAURA SCHOOLCRAFT

Changing It Up

Change **how we relate** to anything, and it will **transform our life**. Our relationships and how we relate form our window to the world. It's how we view life. A simple shift in our perspective on any given subject matter can completely set us free and expand our life, or it can keep us stuck and limit our ability to move forward. What I have come to know is this: any relationship, whether it be a person or any aspect of my life, becomes the story I tell, and that is the way my life will unfold.

Feel It Forward

Take, for starters, the beginning of the day. How many times have you gotten out of bed with a big stretch, feeling and saying, "It's going to be a great day," and, sure enough, it turned out to be a great day? That one simple thought, practiced consistently over time, can allow for and ensure that it is going to be great day! In doing this one simple thing, you have just created a relationship with your day. Thoughts and words have value and power. Feeling your day forward is where the magic begins.

When you can take the time to focus on how every segment of your day will go and actually feel the ease of it, the fun of it, the adventure of what you want, that will be the experience. You will notice the connections that you envisioned were easy, effortless . . . people actually answered your phone calls! You will notice that your schedule came together like a beautiful orchestration, in complete harmony. You surely would notice if that elusive parking spot out front opened up the minute you drove up. This all happened because you set the intention for it to a great day.

"Everything is in perfect timing! There is nothing out of place in my life."

It's About Time

I have always had a difficult relationship to time. There just never seemed to be enough of it. I was always coming from a place of lack. I was always out of time. Late for everything. I could never get everything done that I wanted to do in any given day. I felt overwhelmed by an unending task list. I needed a different relationship to time. I started to say to myself, "There is enough time" and "Everything is in perfect timing." I must have practiced this new thought process for a few short months. Every time the lack of time would show up in my day, I would repeat the phrase "Everything is in perfect timing." *I really began to see how it really was.* If I was late to a meeting because of traffic delays, so was everyone else. Another really helpful tool was to say, "There are no emergencies." This opened every door that seemed to be closed. I would look at all my deadlines, and I would say, "Is this an emergency?" My mind would quickly conclude, "No." It took all the pressure off of me. I actually started to notice that everything in my life was in perfect timing. I would watch as the universe seemed to constantly deliver a perfectly timed harmony of my workday.

Welcome to My Life

No, it didn't just happen overnight. It was not a one-night stand created with a one-time thought. I had built my relationship with the way I want to set my day in motion through a practiced, intentional thought process that consistently produces positive results. This can happen with anything in your life.

We are responsible for our thoughts. I actually never knew that. My parents didn't teach me that, and it surely was not covered in any academic schooling. We actually do have control over our thoughts. We have control over what we listen to. We have control over deciding the people with whom we engage and spend time; this is our choice. We also have a choice of how we think about each person in our life. This shapes our thoughts . . . and our thoughts shape our world.

Awareness of how we relate to things is a key component to creating the life of our dreams. How do we expand our awareness?

Creating Our Life

Once I started having awareness of my thoughts, I realized I was able to pivot any of those thoughts into what I actually wanted: thoughts that made me feel good when thinking them. Over time, I strengthened more of that mindfulness muscle. Today, after eight years, this practice remains a daily focus. I want to feel good! A mindful spiritual practice is essential to feeling good! I am not just talking about meditation, which is a great starting point, but the practice of **gratitude**. Writing down ten things that I appreciate daily has shifted my energy and allowed me to receive all the wonderful things in life.

The Magic of Gratitude

My favorite gratitude practice book is *The Magic* by Rhoda Burns. She sets out twenty-eight different gratitude tools, one per day, to elevate your emotional well-being. This practice will open your energy path, allowing good things to constantly come to you. Viewing life from this positive perspective expands your world. This is law. It is undeniable. The law of attraction is "You get what your think about." I also want to remind you that this law has no discernment of wanted or unwanted thoughts. Law of attraction will give you what you want or what you do not want. Since you have control over your thoughts, why not pick a good-feeling thought? Thoughts of gratitude will shift any relationship with anyone and anything. I encourage you to try this practice for two weeks, consistently, and see your progress. You will notice a huge difference! I have been practicing gratitude for several years now, and it is the one thing that I do not leave home without. I keep that mindful muscle strong. It is my responsibility to make myself as happy as I can be. It is my responsibility to feel good! It is an inside job. No one can do it for me.

Can You Believe It?

What is a belief? Beliefs are just the thoughts that you keep thinking over and over again until you have convinced yourself that they are true. You come to believe it. Rest assured that what you have come to believe is your truth, flawed as it might be. The good news is it can be converted. Your thoughts can be altered to recreate new, improved beliefs. This usually happens at a time when a certain belief no longer serves (meaning "protects") you. Instead of helping to protect yourself, it is now holding you back or even harming you. I call that **a limiting belief:** a thought process that simply does not allow me to have the things I desire and value.

I Do, Do You?

If you think that your husband is a schmuck, and you constantly think about "this idiot I married" in that way of relating to your husband, this man does not have a chance in your world! However, if you start to notice this thought process and start watering the playing field of your marriage with gratitude's mystical powers, you will see a change, an energy shift. Gratitude and appreciation will increase your positive perspective, altering the entire future of your relationship. Gratitude has a snowball effect, growing bigger with the momentum of positive, expanding energy. Even the tiniest mention of appreciation often will provide positive results. When you continue this practice, there will be constant flow and creation of a beautiful, unfolding relationship. It is your choice of how you want to see him.

How Do You Feel?

The feeling that comes from your thoughts is **a telling story**, a sign of whether **your thinking is in alignment or not!** If the feeling is good, your thoughts are aligned with your true self. If the feelings are uncomfortable or fearful, then misaligned thoughts that are not in your best interest exist. Paying attention to how you feel will give you awareness of the changes needed. You can **trust your feelings.** They are there for your guidance. **Feelings are your guidance system.**

"I love thinking about how I relate to certain things that are not working so well in my life. I can easily recreate my perspective. It works like magic!"

Is It Mine, Really?

An important reframing I recently became aware of is my relationship to **"my business."** Just inserting the word *the* instead of *my* before **"business"** can **alter how I relate** to it. When I use the word *my*, then it becomes all-consuming, like it is all about me. It is "my" entire responsibility. I relationally hold or carry too much of the weight. How can I lighten the load of this relationship? Perhaps the answers I might find are solutions allowing others to support the business: vendors, employees, and even partners. How can such a tiny word change my relationship and set me free?

On the Field

I have worked with different **athletes** to support the development and how they **relate to their game**—or "the game." As a mindful coach, I identify their perspective to each different aspect, e.g., their relationship to the coach, their teammates, the referees, the win of the game, their physical health, the ball, the goal, etc. This works well for coaches that see their players operating at their highest potential. The coaches have great belief in their players. This vision elicits the best performance from their players. They see the players in their strengths, skilled and in their magnificence, which supports the players to reach their **highest level.**

Pain Has a Purpose

What is my **relationship to pain**? When my kids were little, my entire focus in life was keeping them from incurring any sort of pain. If, I myself, had a better relationship to pain, I might have allowed them more freedom to express themselves and have been so overprotective at times, it can inhibit their natural development.

I have learned that the simplest form of body pain, like a headache or a stomachache, is just trying to get my attention so I will make the necessary changes. I think it is important for my good health to listen to my body and provide the proper care.

I love knowing it is happening for me!

I admire anyone who can have a good relationship to pain. Football and fighter athletes are my best example of not living in the fear of physical pain. How can they endure one hit after the other? They must know that all pain eventually subsides and, on some level, trust that the body knows how to heal itself. They may have faith that doctors can support their healing. I need that relationship big time! I think I am a wimp to pain!

Parenting Really!

What is **my relationship to "letting go,"** especially with my now adult children? Having the ability to let go of things in my life has been a valuable tool that **creates immediate freedom and serenity**. When I can "let go," it can be a helpful tool to **resolve conflict, especially within myself**. But what if I think that it is my role to fix, have all the answers, and alter every dangerous situation? What if instead, I accept that this is their life and path, and allow them to learn from their own mistakes? **What if I allowed them to effect their own outcomes**? How much more would they **be empowered, building self-esteem while acquiring confidence?** What if I simply got out of the way, embracing the belief that "life is happening for them," for their benefit? I would see the good in everything, not view them as a victim of their decisions.

Who, Me?

To build healthy relationships with others, and to everything in the world around you, it **starts** with setting the foundation of the most important relationship: **the one with yourself.**

What **beliefs** do we have about ourselves? Do we seek fulfillment? What is our contribution to the world? What responsibility do we take for ourselves? Do you have a loving exchange of thought toward yourself? Do you stand up for yourself and honor what is important? Do you constantly judge yourself, making yourself wrong? Do you shame yourself for not completing your work on time or not paying your bills on time? Do you blame yourself for showing up late for appointments, work meetings, or outings with family and friends? These self-judgements hold you in a place of emotional bondage. This habitual thought process can make you feel like there is not solution, not a way out, which I believe is one of the main causes of depression.

The Awareness Gift

Awareness is the strongest building block to any relationship. Meditation has become an essential practice. At first it is difficult to realize the effects of meditation. For change to occur, you must **continually practice** for it to gain momentum. **Awareness is the greatest gift** you will received **from a meditation practice.** Awareness provides a spotlight that illuminates the path of freedom—and true happiness!

Adversity Is a Good Thing?

I view my relationship with the seemly negative difficulties that I encounter as strength training, functioning as a support that creates my personal spiritual growth. Viewing adversity in this way removes all my resistance and clears obstacles I sometimes create. When I make adversity my friend, I can let go, floating down the river of life, and trust the process.

The Art of Relationship

There is an **Art to Relationship.** We are constantly going in and out of connecting with ourselves and others, like a rhythmic dance. Once you master those steps, you are well on your way to having successful relationships.

Every ideal/healthy/successful relationship is built on a strong level of **trust.** Trust takes time through repeated positive actions. I find listening to myself and consistently focusing on self-care are essential trust-builders. I find that when I master trust of myself, I can easily develop trust with others.

A successful relationship **brings a certain level of peace.** A true connection, and a healthy relationship, always starts with being in peace. When you are in fear, anger, or emotional hurt, there is no true connection. Relationships built on these negative emotions will only breed disconnection. Look into the relationship that you have with that conflicting subject. You must come to peaceful and compassionate terms first within yourself. Then you are free to create true connection with others.

In an ideal relationship, there is a restorative process. That process involves someone being heard and listened to when conveying that you only want good for them, and that you care, that they are important. These are the restorative solutions that allow for relationships to thrive.

All we need is love!

Laura Schoolcraft

Laura Schoolcraft is a highly in-demand inspirational speaker on thought creation. Her mission is to intuitively guide our future's great leaders. Her unique perspective will stimulate and challenge your views on life.

Laura's specialty is in transforming new beliefs into manifestations. Her favorite arenas for this are business and athletic development. Growing up, Laura played a number of competitive sports, gaining powerful insights into the world of sports. During high school, she was a Division I softball player with the highest batting average in the nation. She learned to transform untested beliefs into manifested reality. Today, her mission is to elevate athletic development that greatly expands the sport and the players' capacity.

She is a highly skilled life coach who teaches others to develop a valued connection to their true selves. Laura combines her background with her unique ability to mindfully coach athletes from an energetic level. Over the years, Laura has created a daily, systematized mind-strengthening practice to help athletes achieve superior performances. The repetition of this builds the athlete's emotional strength and creates consistent peak accomplishments.

Laura lives in the San Francisco Bay Area with husband, Patrick David, son Kyle, and their adorable dog, Lucy. Her daughter, Danielle, recently married and lives nearby with her husband, Matt, a wonderful, welcomed addition to the family.

Email: **laura.a.schoolcraft@gmail.com**

BUILDING CONNECTION WITH UNLIKELY COMPANIONS
BY JULIA HARRIET

As I pushed open the heavily weathered door, a saloon full of long-bearded miners turned to take me in. Like a scene from a Clint Eastwood movie, the collective conversation dropped, leaving only the echo of a man taking down a foamy gulp of beer. The bartender tipped his wide-brimmed hat as a signal for me to enter. I flashed a reticent smile and walked across the splintered floor toward the only empty stool.

Five days prior, I had packed my car full of journals, crystals, coffee, and my favorite heels with the intent of traversing the Wild West in celebration of the recent launch of my inspirational memoir, *Under Construction: Healing Trauma While Building My Dream*. Having birthed two children of my own, the delivery of my story held no less significance and effort. Within hours of its arrival, *Under Construction* became a #1 international bestseller. Honestly, it still takes my breath away that my words have been so well received by friends and strangers alike. People from around the globe began reaching out to me on social media with supportive messages; with their own sacred stories of healing from trauma.

As I drove down the highway headed south, it slowly began to settle in that I was actually an author of a published book, let alone an impactful one that was making its way into people's hearts around the world.

After taking my seat at the bar, I noted a formidable man standing near the wall, wearing a t-shirt with a black assault rifle stamped across the front. "Come and Take It," the shirt read. It was easy to recognize that perhaps my political, social, and spiritual beliefs differed from the dudes in this bar east of Reno. I grappled with my immediate judgmental response and primal desire to flee from the scene, feeling it may be best to avoid conflict and conversation altogether. But my curiosity drew me towards a place of compassionate inquiry. I wondered what lay beneath these prickly appearances. I wondered, in these times of chaos and opposition, could there be a way through to the hearts of these men? Could we find and nurture the connection innate in us and in our experience of living, loving, and losing as human beings?

"You obviously ain't from around here. But welcome on in. What brings you up here to our little town?"

This wasn't my first rodeo in Virginia City, Nevada. Historically speaking, it was a hub during the Gold Rush days of the mid-1800s, infamous for having a red-light district that rivaled San Francisco, and heralded for being home of the Comstock Lode, the largest silver strike ever discovered in the United States. Nowadays, the colorful locals who ran a handful of bars and antique stores held the tales, trials, and boondoggles of the old days with reverence and enthusiasm. As a lover of oral history, I found myself visiting this mountain town every couple years for a good time and a damn good story.

"I'm on a one-lady tour of the Wild West, and Virginia City is one of my favorite places to visit. I just wrote a book about building my own home during one of the hardest years of my life, and I'm here to have some fun and share in some stories."

A few of the men who hadn't engaged with me at all looked up from their beers and down the bar at me. I recognized this was an opportunity to go from being unknown and out of place to being, if nothing else initially, a source of entertainment.

"I learned through carpentry that we are all under construction— remodeling, making and cleaning up messes, like one crazy project unfolding throughout our lifetimes. Sometimes we get demoed by unfortunate circumstances and have to rebuild from our very foundation, which is what I had to do. None of us can avoid these experiences of pain in life. But we can avoid prolonged suffering. We can awaken into our courage and resilience out of our darkest hours. Especially if we rise up to support and help each other. We are better when we build and grow together, right?"

"Holy shit, did you hear that, guys? We got us a writer in the house! And a builder lady to boot. My wife is always on me to clean up all my damn messes. Now I can tell her not to worry because I'm just under construction. Ha! You see, I'm a heavy machine op and respect a woman who knows her way around a tool box. How long've you been building for? And what's your name, Miss?"

In this moment I noted something profound: within minutes, I had gone from being a stranger in a strange land to being a woman authentically sharing her story with eager recipients. Had I trusted my initial bias construed by the appearances of these men, and vice versa, we would have missed the opportunity to connect and to learn together about what we shared in common. In these times when division seems like the norm in America, it was heartwarming to witness a dissolving of assumption and the desire to bridge our differences with honest intrigue and exploration. Though we all do it, the advice "don't judge a book by its cover" stood its ground.

"My name's Julia Harriet. I'm from a little island up in Washington State, and I've been working in construction for almost six years now. After some searching, I found a contractor who hired me on the spot as a carpentry apprentice even though I couldn't build IKEA furniture. He must have seen my potential. Or at least my passion to learn. Within that first year of apprenticeship, I was already starting to build my own home, which was my life's dream. To build a home with my own hands for my children. And, by God, I've been building ever since. What's your name, so I don't have to call you Mr. Gun Guy?"

A few men chuckled, and I could see that humor was a must as we moved into more vulnerable territory.

"Real nice to be knowin' you, Miss Harriet. I'm Travis. But now, I've gotta ask, what the hell is an IKEA? Sounds like some code word the Soviets would have thought up during the Cold War."

"Nope, it's a Swedish home furniture company that has stores across the U.S. But everything you buy comes in boxes to assemble like a kid's LEGO set. I just meant that I totally sucked at construction when I started. I wanted to become a builder in spite of the steep learning curve. I was determined to build my own home even when I had no property, money, and I kept having things go wrong, and then from wrong to worse. But, according to my dad, I have never done anything the easy way, so deciding to become an apprentice with zero experience was of no surprise to those who know me well."

"You don't look like you ever go through a day without a smile on your face. It's hard to imagine you being dealt a lemon outta life." Travis paused to take a long drink. I took a significant sip of wine myself.

This was the inevitable moment that arose every time in the telling of my story. It's easy to ask strangers to acknowledge my dedication to learn how to build my own house, but telling them about my pain and my loss that occurred during this time required a level of intimacy that made me think. Should I play full out and share vulnerably with a group of conservative, gun-toting miners?

"So, the depth of my smile is the result of what I've overcome. You see, the year I built my house, I went through a divorce while having two small kids, losing my mother to cancer, and being drugged and sexually assaulted in my hometown. In one year, I was completely demoed. I easily could have allowed the pain to define me, to shroud me in silence. But I didn't. While raising the walls of my home, I learned how to rebuild myself, how to rise up out of the ashes, and that's where I found my unwavering joy and strength. That's the smile you see today. It lands on my face but is born from deep within my healing heart."

Mic drop. No one moved. I could see into the men's minds as if I was watching old movie reels of their own experiences of grief, pain, fear, and betrayal. Here we were, together in the unescapable darkness that is married to our very existence. No one could run from it. But also, no one was alone in this moment at this small rural bar.

"Well, you got me impressed by being a builder lady, but now I'm thinking that you're also one hell of fighter. Fighting the good fight for bigger love in this world of hate. I've got two grown daughters who are gonna just love your book. Can I buy a couple off you here and now at the bar? I've got cash money. It'll make a perfect Christmas present for them."

I caught the haggard-looking man to my left at the bar wiping his eyes. He turned, looking out at me from beneath a hedge of eyebrows. "Ma'am, I just wanted you to know that I'm real sorry you had all that loss and hurt. I have been to hell, and it's called Vietnam. All I want these days is for people like you who have courage to go out and let everyone know that they deserve to be happy. I finally got some help a year ago with my PTSD, and I'm getting some sleep again. Just ask Travis here—I am no fun without sleep."

Travis threw his thick hand down on the man's shoulder. "Old Grizzly, as we once called him because he was such a crotchety bugger. But now he's just a sweet old teddy bear, right, Jimmy?"

Travis pinched his leathery cheek hard, and Jimmy let out a hoot and holler at his buddy. The bar let loose with laughter. I looked over at Travis, who was still giggling, and found that in the twinkle of his eye there was the little boy he had once been. I imagined all the men as little boys that were hidden behind wrinkled skin, tattered clothes, long gray beards, and old tattoos. I awakened into the rare beauty of this human exchange. I was no longer seeing these men solely with the critical watch of my eye—I could now experience them through the lens of my heart.

I handed Travis two books with a hug, gave Jimmy and the bartender my business card, and thanked all the men for a most welcome stay at the local saloon.

As I walked down the rickety boardwalk toward my motel room for the night, I held such gratitude for this chance meeting in an old mining town. Humbled by the power of authentic transparency and connection, I wondered what could be possible in our fledgling country if we stopped to see with our hearts. To listen with compassion. To deconstruct the walls we've built that keep us from loving and learning freely. I knew what I had just experienced was no mirage nor miracle. It was the result of awakening to what was really there before me in the hearts of these men. Men who had seen and known hurt. Men who, like me, had been demoed by something and had to figure out how to carry on.

That was when I knew that I needed to bring my story, *Under Construction*, more boldly out to the world to be of service to collective healing. I have the privilege of being a conduit for promoting love over fear, but the experience of how I rebuilt my life belongs to everyone. We all have been dealt a bad hand at times, and we deserve to be held and heard as we reconstruct ourselves. I'm still figuring out how to bring my one-lady tour further out into wilds, just like when I set out on the frontier of building my dream home. **One thing I know is that if I listen to my heart, I will always end up in the right place and time, with people ready to make creative messes, mistakes and pure magic together.**

My name is Julia Harriet, and I'm a survivor. A builder. An advocate. A mother. A lover and friend. I am human. I am now and will forever be Under Construction. How are you under construction? How are you authentically showing up and open to connecting with others in the world?

Julia Harriet

Julia Harriet is a #1 international best-selling author, an inspirational speaker, and a builder who has been working in construction for the past six years on Vashon Island, Washington. She spent a decade teaching everything from preschool to high school art, and she followed her heart that dreamed to one day build her own home for her two beautiful children and began a carpentry apprenticeship at age thirty-five. Julia also volunteers for a local nonprofit in her community, The DOVE Project, to address issues of interpersonal violence in her community.

Julia's recent book, *Under Construction: Healing Trauma While Building My Dream*, became a #1 international bestseller in four countries and a #1 bestseller in nine categories including new release in Happiness. Julia considers herself everyone's builder buddy and loves to support friends and strangers alike in constructing their dreams, no matter what obstacles appear in the way.

juliaharriet.com.
https://www.facebook.com/juliaharriet
IG: julia.harriet.anderson
https://www.linkedin.com/in/juliaharriet

TOUCHED BY LOVE
FROM THE OTHER SIDE
BY ALAN GRENWOOLF

What drives you? What is your purpose in getting up each morning and proceeding through the day only to retire at night, sleep, refresh, and then start all over again the next day? Are you living each day to the fullest, enjoying all the beauty in the warm sun shining on your face, the smell of fresh morning air, or seeing someone with a beautiful smile just for you? What makes your day truly worth living?

With deep thought, these can be challenging questions. Let me tell you about my experience and what I have to share. I hope it will give you a light to steer by, even on the darkest of days.

It all started in 1998 when I first came in contact with my soul mate. At first we didn't know it at the time, but as we got to know each other and shared our stories over the next six months, the more the similarities and synchronicities came about. It was like I was speaking to another me, my other half, literally. We both did some soul searching then and concluded that we were indeed "soul mates." When that statement was verbalized, it was like a chorus of angels said, "Yes, it's about time!" It was so profound at that moment.

From then on, we spent every available moment on the PC talking, sharing, planning, and sending letters back and forth to each other that made our bond that much stronger. In October of 1998, we met physically for the very first time. After much anticipation, I had landed in Seattle at gate N7, the very same gate they used in the movie *Sleepless in Seattle*. I was carrying a rose for her, and she had one for me—that was our signal. We had already sent pictures of each other, so we knew how the other looked. I walked up the ramp and emerged from the doorway seeing her in the short distance away, standing there by herself surrounded by a white light from the large windows on an unusually sunny day. All I could see was her and the flower. Both flowers were the exact same color. Everything else didn't matter. We flew into each other's arms and hugged each other so tightly as she was crying tears, "It's you, it's you!"

I answered, "It's me, it's me!"

And from that point in our lives we never looked back. I went back to my old place, packed my things, and in one month I was in her arms for good.

Later in the spring of 2000, we married and solidified our bond. Over the next years, we experienced life in the traditional sense of working, raising our children, and enjoying the great outdoors. She was a retired registered nurse, always having a deep desire to help people take better care of themselves. She had seen so many things from her old profession that after we met, she went on to become an herbalist, and with my farming and sales background we started our own herbal business. We traveled all over the state selling our products and meeting so many new and enlightened people who were like-minded as us.

We became stronger together spiritually, too, learning new modalities and other items of interest. We both became Reiki masters, which opened the doorways to many other paths. That has helped me so much over time. We even had a Reiki circle that we hosted once a week and taught some others the path of Reiki energy. The shamanic practices called to me, in which I studied with those. My wife, we found out, was an empath, which led us on more new beginnings. Combining our talents and everything together, we were happy and helped many folks, more than we could ever imagine.

More time had passed, and we made a move to the eastern side of the state. We lived there for ten years and expanded our herbal business before moving back to our old area after we found out my wife had breast cancer for the second time.

Our experiences and life were wonderful, looking back on the past. With the cancer, she "lived a quality, not quantity life," as she called it. We dealt with all kinds of obstacles and faced many viewpoints from others in how we needed to handle our situation, but, being herbalists and strong to our nature, we decided to go the natural route and live with dignity and wholesomeness to honor her values. After a valiant ordeal, she went home three years later.

Always optimistic, not one moment was spent in thinking about the end and that she would be living on forever, conquering all of our doubts. Looking back during those three years, it gave us the time to arrange all of our affairs and all the needed elements for me to proceed after her departure. Life opened the doors for needed events to happen in synchronicity, allowing everything to be accomplished at the right time. I spent every moment of every day taking in all the memories we could manage.

We lived a lifetime in just twenty-two-plus years. Most folks would have thought that our lives together were over. I sure did, even with all my beliefs, but with her "going home," **life didn't end there!** In fact, our lives just kept going, opening new chapters in both of our lives.

Opening the last chapter of my life here on Earth, I dealt with, argued with, and cried until I dried up inside with *grief* for my beloved. Grief grabbed me like no other enemy has ever had a grip on me before. Through many trial-and-error scenarios, I found out the hard way that grief is not only a necessary pathway to travel through but that it is purely for your own body's mechanisms and not for your soul's purpose. After living a certain way for so long, your body has to go through a detox of sorts because it's not receiving all of the endorphins, feeling sensations, positivity, and security from your spouse. Grief affects every sense of the body in so many ways. Your sight, touch, smell, hearing, and feeling the energy of your loved one has come to a screeching halt, and your body doesn't know what to do. I didn't.

What I didn't know at the time was just how close to me she really was. Two or three weeks after her going home, she came to me in a vision of loveliness, showing her form to me. It was as real as if I stood in front of you. Seeing her, standing in the doorway to our place, she showed me many things. It was only for a moment, but it was just long enough to let me see her and take it in. She was so beautiful and youthful-looking, "healed" from the cancer and smiling so lovingly in her angelic form.

After her appearance, she started coming to me more often, speaking to me and telling me things like "Get back into your spirituality" and "You must continue on for the both of us." Taking her advice, I did so. Doors opened up for me more than ever before. I was noticing synchronicities much more often and how everything started falling into place without lifting a finger. Messages from Spirit, and from her, poured into my consciousness. I was told to "let go" so many times. **I wrestled with those ideas of having to let go of her and her memories when, later, I pieced together that it was a letting go of what was—our old life—in order to make room for** *our new life together.*

My digging around found many more synchronicities which have guided me to my destination now. **When I had learned to get out of the way and trust that Spirit has your back, all things are possible.** I was led to websites that provided the needed answers I was looking for, courses to help with my subsiding grief and also lifting my spirit. I learned the art of mediumship and how to communicate more clearly with "the other side."

Through adventures with my beloved on our psychic journeys, I found answers to many of my questions of existence without her here. I was supposed to be the one who was left behind in this lifetime. In previous lives, I was the one who usually went home first. She was the one who mostly had to endure the grief and resulting life. We also found out that this experience had cut some lingering karmic ties we had, which were mostly attached to me. I found out what true grief was, what letting go really meant. I found out just how deeply I love this woman and that it is an eternal element of our lives. I know that it will never cease. I found the experience of **unconditional love,** a love so profound and so meaningful that it percolates in the bones of my soul. Her going home granted me these experiences, to better **our soul's purpose** all because it was my turn to stay behind this time around.

Quite unintentionally, I had developed a deep feeling inside of me that needed to be fulfilled, one that I can only attribute it to my wife, and that was **journaling**. I found out that the more I could write about her, even though it hurt like heck, the more I healed inside for the next day. I wanted a solid remembrance of those events that were happening. I also wanted to write down things of our past while I thought of them. This was my saving grace for my sanity at the time, as I had already started to forget some of those important memories. This wasn't discovered until I was rereading one of my journals and the proof of its benefits was being read back to me.

On one day of my journaling, my next level of progression stepped forward as I heard her sweet voice over my shoulder say, "This would make a great book." That statement started me into writing with more earnest, finding out that I dearly loved it. It has become a part of me now that feels so right.

One of our favorite sayings that has been passed on to us from our Reiki masters and has always stuck with the both of us over the years goes like this. "**We are not physical beings having a spiritual experience, but rather we are spiritual beings having a physical experience**." Heaven is not in the clouds in some faraway place. Each person has their own perspective on exactly where it is and how it looks. But, in my opinion, Heaven is all around us and here on Earth as well, behind a veil of forgetfulness.

I remember one incident during a Reiki circle. We had a gentleman hop up onto the table, and as I started working on him, I noticed something quite unusual. So I called over one of our trainees to work on this man's lower leg.

I asked if she noticed anything unusual or different about his leg. "What kind of energy do you feel?"

"Nothing, it seems normal to me," was the reply.

I said, "Good. Then we'll proceed."

I saw she had a quizzical look on her face. When we finished the session and I had the gentleman sit up, then I posed the question: "Sir, can you tell me about your leg?"

"Yes, well, I lost it in an accident . . ." and he went on telling us all about it.

Our trainee's mouth dropped opened without a sound.

"That is why we treat the whole person!"

Physically his leg was not there, but energetically it still was, thus still needing the attention of the Reiki energy. I use this example because it is the same with us as souls, I believe. We are still here, having gone through the transition, only we in the physical world are not able to see them with our own eyes. They are in another "dimension of viewing" that is only visible with our minds' eyes and through our intuition.

We have lived many lifetimes over as souls. We keep coming back to this wonderful Earth to reconnect, learn new experiences, and relearn old experiences until we get it right. For our continuation in the evolution of our souls, we must strive to get it right in order to evolve into our next level of existence as eternal beings. This is only a "speed bump" in time compared to the lifetime of our souls. **We are also the messengers for others who are unable to make this type of journey, and all of this is generated by our love for each other. Love is what makes everything possible.**

For me, I am still healing from all of this. How can one not be? Gone are the days of normal, but there is a new normal now, one for the future to start again with new goals. There is no going back now, just forward. Although my wife and I are physically apart, I am still in communication with her almost on a daily basis. We talk together like she is right here beside me, and, in truth, she is. She has shown me on many journeys that Heaven is closer to us than we think and more beautiful than we can imagine.

Why do I get up each day? So I can become the Lightworker for those who need help. To see, once again, the "smile that is just for me." The love of my family and close friends shows me that every day. It's about "us," the Spirit Warriors, to continue on lighting the way and using our gifts, reminding everyone who we truly are . . . spiritual beings having a physical experience.

I am writing a series of books titled *I Am Home*. It tells of my transformational journey with my beloved wife's "going home" and what it has been like for me since then. With an autobiography of our physical lives together in the first book, it explains and tells of the many confirmations I received and how we can work with spirits on the "other side" for the betterment of all. Then, in the ensuing books, we take off in "actual spirit journeys of the soul." They are uplifting and inspirational along with adventures that are pure and wholesome compared to what is being presented nowadays.

Come visit me at www.alangrenwoolf.com to learn more. I am also on Facebook, Twitter, and Instagram for those too. Look for Alan Grenwoolf. If I can be a spark of inspiration for you to help find your way, I would be glad to share. **Remember to smile for someone special in your life today—it just may change their world!**

Alan Grenwoolf

Alan Grenwoolf is a spiritual mentor, teacher of energy medicine, and author who chose his mission to carry on the Spirit of his work and to help walk along with those who are searching for their own healing path who may be grieving from a loved one. Not long ago, with his wife's "going home," he has personally travelled the long road to recovery and found his true life's path, answering his call from Spirit to lead others on their own pathways of discovery. He would like to share his process and the steps he took to ultimately live on, open your world to recovery, and help release you from the "chains of burden" that you may or may not be aware you are carrying and to rediscover one's self, finding life with purpose once again. Breathe in that fresh air again, and truly live your life as it was intended, with purpose.

He is coming forward with his experiences of a lifetime as a Reiki master, shamanic practitioner, and minister as well as a naturalist, herbalist, and a lover of happiness. He is the author of four manuscripts, the *Love Beyond* series, that are currently in their production stages right now. Come and journey with him on the links below. Namaste.

Email: **alangrenwoolf@gmail.com**
Website: **alangrenwoolf.com**
Facebook: **Alan Grenwoolf**
Twitter: **@alangrenwoolf**
Instagram: **alangrenwoolf**

PART THREE

CHANGE IN ACTION

"If your actions inspire others to dream more, learn more, do more and become more, you are a leader."
—John Quincy Adams

HOW I BECAME
THE GODDESS OF JOY
BY ROBYN VIE CARPENTER

"'Goddess of Joy'? Don't you feel like calling yourself a goddess is a bit self-aggrandizing?" That's the question a friend of mine asked ten years ago when I chose my Twitter handle. It kind of set me back on my heels. For the record, I'm @GoddessofJoy almost anywhere you look on social media, including my YouTube channel. Funny thing is, although I deflected my friend's question at the time, it actually stayed with me for years. Was I being self-aggrandizing? Who was I to call myself a goddess? The other funny thing is, I never changed it. Now that I've had it for so long, I kind of feel as though it became a self-fulfilling prophecy. Even though it felt I had been it all along. The journey to stepping into this moniker was filled with love, laughter, tears, and a lot of self-affirmation. This is how I become the "Goddess of Joy."

Ten years ago I was facing the end of a job, then a relationship, and losing my home all in a matter of five months' time. It was one of those times that you look back at and marvel at how great the lessons really were—if you do your work.

July 2011, at four years and 360 days, I lost my job. Two days later, I, and my then-girlfriend, got evicted. So, with only two days left in the month, I took my severance pay, with a letter from unemployment, and secured a new place for us to live.

September 2011, my "why do we have to put a label on it" girlfriend of five-plus years found love, and it wasn't with me. I was denied unemployment and had been working for my now-ex at the time. So I lost my love and my only source of income all at one time. I begged and borrowed and wrote people's term papers (really) in order to pay that month's rent.

October 2011, I kind of imploded and moved out. I moved back to my parents' house. I did a lot of journaling and a lot of crystal realignments on my energetic body. Things I had been studying for years. Things that I forgot that I even knew. Things that I never knew that I knew. I did everything I could. I worked all of my personal magick on me for a change. I gratefully had an amazing support system of friends and family that enveloped me with love. I received aura cleansing. I had tarot readings. I got back into yoga. At the end of the month, I attended a Witches' Ball and danced until my soul felt free. I experienced an incredible number of psychic encounters with multiple people and had someone fall to their knees and call me "My Goddess"! It was a very good night. The first thing I did was move back into my apartment. I felt empowered and renewed. I literally felt as though I was coming out of a fog. Someone that had seen me within days of the breakup saw me again in October, and they said, "You looked gray the last time I saw you. Now you look vibrant and alive." Clearly, my magic was working.

This gave me the energy I needed to restart my small business consulting company. I had been operating a consulting business for a few years helping small business owners think differently about what it really means to be an entrepreneur. However, it became clear very soon after I had my first coffee meeting with a new potential client that I was no longer supposed to be having conversations with them about their business. I was being led to having deeper conversations about their spiritual life. I found myself discussing with people the way I did my ceremony and rituals, and how I journal. I found myself dancing in the living room and making soup for my friends instead of doing all of my usual hustle to find the money things. I wasn't worried. I knew I could figure something out.

November 2011, no money for rent. I tell my ex that she has to come to get her stuff. My name is on the lease, my hustle and severance have been paying the rent. I declared, "I'm making this my space." I was getting by on a stipend from an associate producer/set goddess gig I got. It felt like a combination of my life from when I first moved home after I left the East Coast, with my life when I was living my city-girl dreams in New York City. This time, I had friends, support, and my own place! I was still finding my voice and exploring my freedom. I set some boundaries that really needed to be set. I told my ex that I was no longer holding space for her to come back to me. I started walking almost every day at the park and then having meetings with people to see if something sparks about my "what's next."

I did *a lot* of journaling. I wrote about visions I had. Feelings I was feeling, songs that were inspiring me. I wrote poetry. I hadn't written poetry in years. I then came to the realization that I was living in the exact neighborhood that I said I wanted to live in when I first moved back to Denver eight years before. Then, *look*, there I am doing a ceremony at midnight on a rooftop during a lunar eclipse. I begin to realize that although I hadn't quite worked out the money, my life is beginning to feel like what I knew it could feel like. I was becoming the kind of person I always said I wanted to be. I felt like a "me" I had almost forgotten existed. I also found a "me" I never realized existed. I was bold and vocal about my wants, needs, and desires. I was beginning to feel confident in my ability to be the "me" that I knew that I was here to be. I was expressing the joy that I was experiencing. I found myself at the beginning of a new vision.

December 2011, I get another eviction notice. This is the second time in less than five months I received one. I was more disappointed about the second one. I finally felt free of so much fear and filled with so much effervescent light, I couldn't understand why it wasn't working out financially so that I could stay. The thing is, I knew deep within me that everything would be all right. At the same time, good things were happening. I got my sexy back. I felt powerful. I had even begun to wear my hair in its natural state, a mass of curls all over my head. My friend calls it my "power hair." And, honestly, releasing myself from all of the hair-straightening rituals literally gave me hours back in my week and a feeling of empowerment that I find difficult to put into words. So I call it my "empowered hair."

And then it happened, in quick succession. I have an energetic realignment that I can only describe as if my lower chakras turned and clicked into place. That evening while leading a prayer circle, someone observed that I was glowing. They said that there was a glow to my face that seemed like it was coming from within instead of on the surface of my face. Then I found myself at lunch with a friend, and she asked the question that really changed everything: "If you could do anything, money no object, what would you do?" Have you ever asked yourself that? I asked my brother-in-law once, and he said, "Clean pools." I think it was the farthest away that he could think of from the office that he was sitting in. What would you do if you didn't have to worry about how much money you made?

My answer was a revelation. "I would travel the world teaching people how to connect to their joy."

I can honestly say that this answer had never come out of my mouth before. I had never once expressed to myself or anyone else that I had a desire to teach joy. I didn't even realize that I had any feeling or opinion about joy, right up to the moment I said it.

"How are you going to do that? How will people even know who you are to realize that they need you to teach that to them?" Once I had made my statement, my friend had several follow-up questions. Her master's degree is in law; she always has a lot of clarifying questions.

"I don't know. That wasn't the question. Maybe I'll write a book," I said. I was not daunted because once I had said it, I knew it was true. I really do want to travel the world teaching people how to connect to and live a life of joy. Even though I had never said it before, I recognized it as "my truth" the moment I uttered the words. I immediately started journaling about it. I had been working on book ideas for years. I had at least two half-completed books. This idea of teaching people about joy really grabbed hold of me.

So, I was still being evicted, although I was finally finding inspiration for my "what's next." Since I didn't have any immediate prospects for cash, I decided that I would move out and not even fight to keep this "perfect apartment" because I realized it wasn't perfect because I didn't know how I was going to pay for it. The court date was coming up, but I couldn't face going to hear them tell me to vacate. I just prayed that I would be okay until after Christmas.

I did in fact get a reprieve until after Christmas, and literally the moment that I was putting the last of the items in my friend's car is the moment the sheriff pulled up to put the note on my door. I have a picture of me in that empty apartment that last day smiling joyfully because so much good came from being there.

Following those eventful months, I had what I call an "eat, pray, love" year. I kept working on myself. I only worked with a couple of clients. I did a lot of work around family and really fully embraced myself as a member of my family in a way that I never had before. I found myself at a spiritual center to attend service, and I began attending classes and programs. I discovered a path I wanted to pursue academically. I was still getting clear on what I really helped people with. As I learned, I became a better teacher. I knew when it was working because I could see it in my students' faces. I also knew when it wasn't working because I wasn't having fun. I started a blog, which is why I started the Twitter account. The blog was called *The Joy of Being You*. It was based on the book I was writing. Remember the book? I spent almost five months writing the book longhand. You read that right. I wrote the entire book by hand. Then I typed it out and gave it to two people. Then I started writing a blog because my friend Linda Villarosa, a writing professor at City College and author of many books, told me that people were going to need to find me and read my stuff before any publisher was going to believe that someone would want to read a book I wrote. So I started to write.

When I started, it really was because I "needed to create content." Very quickly, I realized how much I missed it. I had dreamed of being a writer when I was fourteen. I wrote, and people read it. I started my Twitter account and pretended to myself that I believed I was a Goddess of Joy. I found out that people were finding my writing from all kinds of places. And then there I was, at my friend's World Cup viewing party, talking in a group of people, and I mentioned the blog. "Wait. You write that blog?" she said. "Yes. You've read it?" I asked. "That blog changed my life." Yep. That actually happened. I immediately went outside and called my mother in joyful tears! "Mummy, it's working!" She said what she always said: "I'm so proud of you!" I also found out that editors from the local LGBTQ paper had been reading. They offered me a columnist position that I immediately accepted! Life was good and very good! I was feeling my Self in ways I had always dreamed I could be. I couldn't imagine how much better it would get.

At almost a year to the day from when my ex left me, I met the woman that would later become my spouse. I call her my wusband. I could write a volume about all of the wonderful things she has been in my life. This is the point of her being here in my story. She arrived the moment I knew that my life would be "fine and dandy" if I didn't meet her. Once I didn't need someone to want me in order to prove my value to myself, I found someone that is constantly proving she believes in me and is proud to support me in every way she is able. She's the only person, regardless of gender, that my father has ever believed was worthy to take care of me. Which is weird high dad praise, haha!

Each year since the fall of 2011, I marvel at the goodness that my life has offered me. I listened to the voice within me, telling me to be my biggest, brightest Self. I found a spouse that says the same thing. So, I decided that every dream that I've ever dreamed was possible if I still wanted it. That's why, in the fall of 2017, *Let's Get Stoned: Using Stones and Crystals to Create a Life That Rocks!* was released. My dream of writing a book was finally realized. It was a journey of believing that I really did have something to teach and share. It's about living a life of joy, knowing that it's a choice, and understanding that stones and crystals can be a powerful tool to help you create the life you want: a life that rocks!

As I sit here writing this, I've been married for eight years, I'm a certified life coach and in my first year of internship for my Spiritual Practitioner license. My book is still being discovered and regularly sells out at local bookshops across the country. I'm already working on the research outline for my next book and the editing notes for the second edition of *Let's Get Stoned*. If you google me, you'll see a lot of pictures from the last ten years. You'll notice I'm laughing in most of them. When I decided to become a Goddess of Joy, I also decided that meant I had to live a life of joy. The best part is, this is what I help my clients learn how to do. My goddess power is inspiring you to choose joy daily.

Remember, my friends, you are "illimitable"! This means you can create whatever you want. So why not create a life that rocks?

Robyn Vie Carpenter

Robyn Vie-Carpenter is a certified life coach, a certified laughter yoga instructor, and is currently a Licensed Spiritual Practitioner candidate with Heart and Soul Center of Light in Oakland, California. Her book *Let's Get Stoned: Using Stones and Crystals to Create a Life That Rocks!* was released in fall of 2017. This self-proclaimed Goddess of Joy has clients all over the country while making her home in Baton Rouge, Louisiana.

You can follow Robyn on Instagram and Twitter as @Goddessofjoy, visit her business Facebook page www.facebook.com/goddessofjoyrvcb, and watch over fifty videos on her YouTube channel, https://youtube.com/c/GoddessofJoy.

OWNING MY LEADERSHIP STORY
BY DR. BETH HALBERT

Today, I claim I am an awakened leader. It took me a long time to get here. For much of my life, I told myself I was not enough, I was not "there" yet, and that there was so much more I was "supposed" to do. I saw a huge gap between the desire to be an Awakened Authentic Powerful Feminine World Leader and actually being one (or becoming one). At times I even felt like a total loser, a failure, and a fraud.

Then one day in 2018, in front of over sixty people in a workshop, I claimed, by writing on a big flip chart: "I am an authentic powerful feminine world leader —signed Beth Halbert." The rest of 2018 until now, I've been doing things in my business and my life to live into that flip-chart-sized sign that is now hanging over my office desk.

In 2018, I had already paid a business coach $40K to get me there and instead ended up an additional $60K in debt, which seemed impossible at the time to pay off. To make a long, sad story short, I decided to let go of my story and move toward what I wanted instead of fighting for my limitations.

So I asked myself, "What do I do, Dr. Beth?" I started looking through my own tools and became my own inner coach, mentor, partner, and cheerleader.

I have created a tool to transform anything that is no longer serving me. I call it *The 10 Keys to Compassion*. Find it at this link: www.drbeth.com/freestuff. This process transformed my life, and I hope it is supportive of you and your journey.

Key 1 : Compassion Falling in love with what is, where I am, and loving who I am in every given moment. This was a difficult place to start. My Inner Teen was in full force—in a No Compassion mode. I called it "swimming through the deep end of the vomit pool." I came to a point in which I prayed that if this was really as far as I could make it to being a next-world leader, then I'm out! I told myself, "Go ahead and take me, God. I've had a good life, I've talked a good game, I've gone as far as this road will take me."

To make matters worse, I paid to participate in a once-a-month TV show. I remember the week I could not even pretend to have it together and pretend I was having FUN (my signature motto is "If it's not fun, it just doesn't get done"!). The only way I could play full out was to be authentic. So, I wore my pajamas and used the f-word a few times. I think it may have been one of my best presentations yet. LOL!

I journaled about this whole incident and read this first part to my mom. She said, "Oh no, don't tell them that," trying desperately to protect my image. She suggested I instead tell them about all the people who love me and the lives I've saved, etc. I so appreciated her intentions, and by extension all other parents who try to protect their children in this way.

What most of us hear, or make up, when we are "critiqued" for telling our truth is that it's not safe to be me. It's not safe to tell the truth. And this is where leadership feels like the lone lead bird at the head of the flock, ready and willing to be taken down.

What I've learned is that it's really only me who can love, accept, encourage, have faith in me and choose to become an Authentic Powerful Feminine World Leader. I've also learned it's a journey, not a destination. Every minute of every day, I have the choice to either comply with past patterns, past leadership ideas, and past lessons or to live into my own authentic internal spiritual guidance system, or choose to step more fully into my truth.

Sometimes we are cut down, critiqued, silenced by those who love us and who want to protect us the most. We can choose in those moments to own that position from the bottom of your heart. It takes consistency, commitment, and conscious choice to keep choosing love. Keep choosing to be your authentic self. And keep choosing to be visible even in the face of discomfort, the pandemic, the unknown, and constantly moving forward to the best of your ability.

I believe the most important step I can ever take is to know myself in each moment. To honor myself. To acknowledge, to care, listen and to take care of my Inner Family first. (See below for more on my Inner Family.) This has been my lifelong journey and it is sometimes easier said than done. On the days I succeed, where I am filled up from within, I have immense courage, love, and energy to be of service and to help others become their own awakened, powerful next-world leader.

While I was writing this chapter, doctors found a spot in my left breast, and I awaited the results of the biopsy. It was time to have one of those courageous moments. So, I asked myself, "Dr. Beth, how do you get through this?"

First, I journaled with all my "little ones." "Little b" (my inner three-year-old) said she was scared. "Super b" (my inner seven-year-old) said she was super scared. "Bubblin B" (my inner teen) said she was scared shitless! Interestingly enough, before I asked each one of them how they were, I did not feel any fear and was walking around feeling pretty strong and courageous, like "I've got this!" Then I decided to journal more with what else was not present. (As an Awakened Leader, it's our job to gather information, both inside and out.)

Second, I decided to journal and talk with the spot on my breast. She said, "I'm raging mad!" I wondered, where was that rage hiding? Curiously, I was present to feeling love, joy, bliss, and happiness. The spot explained that she was angry and judging other "awakened leaders" for not being willing to work through the hard stuff with other "awakened leaders." Many people who have challenges with others choose to leave instead of working things out. The spot said, "When love gets hard the hardened get going."

As I continued my journaling and expressed critical judgment and condemnation of my most awakened, loving spiritual mentors, I knew I would immediately choose to own **Key 2: Mirror Mirror**. Anything and everything I saw in my external reflection, I would choose to love and find within myself.

Third, I journaled and asked myself, "What part of me would like to die?" I believe awakened leaders ask the hard questions, the questions most people avoid. What I heard amidst the rage and thoughts about dying was that it felt scary and alone to be the lead bird of my life. I wanted others to "play my way" or I would take my toys and go home! ("My way" is to own all our triggers, all our reflections, all our judgments, basically anything and everything we see in another.)

Many people are writing about 5-D. They claim we are moving from the individual blame-shame game to unity, love, win-win, etc. I've been engaging in aspects of 5-D since I was a trainer/facilitator at Saturn (the car company) more than thirty-five years ago, bringing in the new game concepts of Win-Win-Win.

My current mission is to expand my Dr. Beth bubble out into the rest of the world. I want the awakened leaders I know, as well as my loving peers and my mentors, to be by my side. I want them to play my Own Your Story game with me to a level that the vast majority do not want to even entertain.

As a result of this wanting to die and the rage and judgment I was feeling, I took myself through the 10 Keys to Compassion journey with my journaling...

Key 1, Compassion—Falling in love with myself exactly where I am and not judging myself no matter what.

Key 2, Mirror Mirror—If I see it in another, I'm willing to get curious and look for where I might be doing the same thing to myself.

Key 3, Own Your Story—Identify what I'm telling myself to be my "truth" and then decide if I want to continue to live into that story or create and write a more fun story to live out the rest of my days.

Key 4, Playful Messy—Be willing to ask hard questions; see, name, and express the blasphemous; listen to and play full out from within and without.

Key 5, Affect—Feel all my feelings and name them out without acting them out on someone else's head!

Key 6, Self-Care—Put my oxygen mask on first, literally and figuratively. Take care of myself inside (my Inner Family emotional states) and outside (my body and all my physical aspects).

Key 7, Self-Trust—I can say anything to myself knowing that I am heard, loved, and cared for, if by no other, then at least by me and my Divine Inner Self.

Key 8, Intrinsic Into Extrinsic—I am looking at everything I'm seeing in my body and what I might believe is living into my reality, as well as an awareness and willingness to be wrong, change my mind, and live into what I consciously desire and dream about.

Key 9, Organize Your Village—I am listening to my inner village (my inner children and my inner emotional states) as well as my outer village (my friends, family, doctors, nurses, healers, etc.).

Key 10, kNOw My Boundaries—I am identifying what I'm willing to do and what I'm not willing to do when it comes to my body, life, business, and dreams.

<u>I then started my Inner Family Journaling process with the 10 Keys at my side.</u>

> *Dang, I am having some big feelings this a.m. I was talking with the spot, and she said she wants attention and is raging mad. One of my spiritual mentors said it is about being open to and willing to receive. I have had a story that receiving has strings, contracts, agreements, paybacks, attachments, etc. And yes, I can see that beautiful young mirror in me. (Key 5, Affect; Key 3, Mirror Mirror)*
>
> *What part of me would like to get cancer and die? (Key 4, Playful Messy)*

Maybe the first person that ever can actually stand in the fire with me is me. Is there anyone who wants to stand in the fire and own all that they see, all that they make up about what they see, AND all that others make up about what they see in you? This Awakened Leaders Journey is not for the faint of heart!! (Key 4, Playful Messy)

I feel so alone and feel like if I take in support, I have to give support that I may or may not have to give in any given moment. Roosters may come to roost when I don't have the money or energy to pay up. (Key 2, Own Your Story—how's that story working for me?)

Ok, am I wrong? Am I pushing my agenda? Am I making "them" bad and wrong for being where they are? I fear if we the "spiritually aware, the 'awakened' ones" are not able and willing to get through the tough times with each other, then I'm not sure how this world will progress during these times. It makes me challenge whether I even want to be an awakened leader—to be the lead bird on some of these out-there concepts, constructs, or teaching points. (Key 9, Organize Your Village; Key 10, kNOw Your Boundaries)

The good news is that it only takes one of us to do this construct at a time. And I'm even willing to do it all of the time, AND I'm not thrilled about being the only one willing to play. (Key 8 Intrinsic into Extrinsic and Key 2 Own Your Story)

I think it's going to take all of us working together or at least a few of us choosing to be awake, aware, and willing to Own, Love, and Listen to All of what we see in ourselves and each other.

My journaled projections: Everyone wants everyone else to do their work. Mirror: I want everyone else to do my work too. Spiritual leaders quit and leave when it gets uncomfortable, hot, not fun. Mirror: I also want to leave and quit when it gets uncomfortable, hot, and not fun.

Common Wisdom: I can hear focus on what I WANT, not what I don't want. Focus on what's working, not on what's not working. Focus on gratitude, not on victimhood, judgment, and blame. And yet with my big, huge feelings in this moment, my take is I'm willing to work together or "peace out," I want to quit too.

To enjoy more journaling entries, go here: www.DrBeth.com/freestuff

The main point I want you, the reader, to get from this chapter is to know that you are not alone. You can choose your focus. Also, you are welcome to become a part of my Compassion Village tribe. In this community, you will understand that YOU are the leader you are waiting for. I am looking for people who want to share with and play with me and others at this level, and who know that everything they see, create, and receive comes from the inside out.

Who are you? What old story are you sticking to? What new story and truth are you claiming? And what game are you willing to play as we create our next chapter? I would love to invite you to join my tribe to identify your story and then decide if you want to stick to that story or create and own a new one that you can live into for the rest of your life. Here is the link to join my tribe and share your story: www.DrBeth.com/freestuff

I look forward to profoundly playing with you! Don't forget to take great care of yourself first!

Beth Halbert

Dr. Beth Halbert, a.k.a. DrBeth, known as "America's Teenologist," has a thirty-plus-year history working as a corporate trainer, keynote speaker, executive coach, educator and consultant for family-owned businesses and Fortune 500 companies. She has a thriving private clinical psychology practice, facilitates national workshops for parents and teens, and delivers highly educational and extremely entertaining keynote presentations.

DrBeth is committed to creating sustainable social change and supporting people to become the leaders they want to be. Among her clients are American Family Insurance, Cadillac, General Motors, Honda, J.D. Power and Associates, Marriott, McGraw Hill, Toyota, and Volkswagen. She has also been featured on more than two hundred nationally syndicated television, radio, newspaper, and magazine outlets.

As a licensed child psychologist and expert with teens, parents, teachers, health professionals, and others, DrBeth has worked with thousands of families and "first responders" to create stronger parent–teen bonds. She takes a unique approach to helping families overcome the difficulties of adolescence, combining proven clinical practices with warmth, playfulness, self-expression, love, and compassion. She knows how teens think and act and gets them to talk about their emotions and behaviors. She also knows strong-willed adults and gets them to accept themselves exactly as they are and accept their children and others exactly as they are.

In short, DrBeth fully understands human behavior, relational dynamics and "inner family" dynamics (including our inner three-year-olds, our inner seven-year-olds, and our inner teens). She works closely and compassionately with people of all ages, supporting them to appreciate themselves, engage in positive dialogue with others, and develop healthy, connected, loving relationships in especially challenging, dysfunctional situations.

Email: **DrBeth@DrBeth.com**
Cell phone: (925) 403-4113 (textable)
Website: **DrBeth.com**
Facebook: **www.facebook.com/drbethcp**
https://www.facebook.com/DrBethTeenologist
https://www.facebook.com/groups/1498857563603184
(Double Dog Dare Challenge group)
LinkedIn: **https://www.linkedin.com/in/drbeth**
Twitter: DrBethCP **http://twitter.com/DrBethCP**
YouTube: DrBethCP **www.youtube.com/user/drbethcp**
Instagram: DrBethH: **https://www.instagram.com/drbethh**
Pinterest: DrBethCP: **https://www.pinterest.com/drbethcp/_saved**

JOURNEY TOWARDS WHOLENESS
BY RIYA WANG

The Calling

I heard a voice from inside my head, a voice kept telling me, "Go, go, you need to get out here. You need to go to Tibet. There is something there you need to connect with." Go to Tibet? Why? What is this? Who is in my head telling me to go to Tibet?

Who and how am I going to connect? What about my business? How about the life I have built here in America? Yes, it's true, I am not happy. Yes, I am stressed out with my business. Yes, my health is falling apart. It seems everything in my life is about chaos.

It's was close to the middle of the night. Everyone had left a few hours ago. I was still sitting in my favorite big green chair at my office. I turned off my computer and closed my eyes for a few minutes. When I opened my eyes again, I looked around through my big glass door, my beautiful Day Spa in front of me. The lights are warm and inviting, the tall ceiling with the beautiful paper color is calm. My favorite wood painting was hanging in the middle of the wall. The yellow roses at the reception desk looked so beautiful. My clients would always see me at this beautiful spa that seemed so relaxed, and I made my life in society's eyes sound amazing and successful.

I closed my eyes again and took a deep inhale. I try to push out my thoughts that are overwhelming me, but the memories are overflowing in my head.

My life is like a dramatic movie. Scene after scene playing in my head.

When I was born, my parents sold me. I never got a chance to know them or ask why they didn't want me.

I was lucky that my adoptive father gave me so much love, but he died when I was thirteen. That was the first time my heart felt broken. After my father died, the following year, I finished middle school. My mom told me that we didn't have money for me to continue high school. I would need to go to work to make money to take care of my family. I started full time work at age fifteen years old. That year, my mom was upset with me so she did not talk to me for three months. I felt sad, lonely, and helpless. I believed that after my father was gone no one in this world would love me

Finally, I left my mom, left home when I was seventeen. On my own for the first time I told myself I wanted to change my life. Just how I would change my life, I didn't know. I went to a new city where I didn't know anyone and I didn't speak the language. But I knew in my heart I would survive. I slept under a bridge for a few days before I finding my first job in that city.

Struggling to survive in the strange city by myself and dealing with the fact that my biological parents sold me because of the fact that I was a girl was challenging. I thought there must be something wrong with me, that I was worthless, that no one wants me, and no one will ever loves me. I felt so lonely and sad, my world was crushed. My life was not even worth living. No one would care if I died. I tried to kill myself at age twenty-four. I didn't succeed, as you know now. But I needed a reason to live. Soon I found an important reason: I had a short marriage and I had a daughter with my first husband. He never worked during our marriage years. When my daughter turned three, I became a hard-working single mom.

By working hard, I built a successful business at the age of thirty. I had two spas, a coffee shop, a clothes store, and a company with over thirty employees. I started to take care of my mom, my brother and the whole family. It seemed my life was better, and that finally I became a successful woman in China. My daughter needed me, my family needed me. That was my value, I kept telling myself.

Life Takes Other Turns

I married again at age thirty-four. My daughter was seven. I married my second husband, who was an American so he was from foreign country and grew up in a totally different culture than my own. Even though we didn't speak each other's language, we had love and passion.

After we married, he quit his job. He told me he hated being an English teacher and was unable to find other jobs in China since he didn't speak Chinese. So, I took care of him while we lived in China for a year and half until we eventually moved to America.

I sold all my business and moved to California. Seven months after we moved, my husband left my daughter and me. That day I still remember what he said to me: "You are the perfect wife, but I don't need a wife anymore." I cried and I asked him, if he felt any responsibility for my daughter and me after we moved to this country with him as a family.

He said as he left, "I didn't put a gun on your head to ask you to come with me." Each part of the words deeply burned my heart.

After he left, I felt abandoned again. My heart was broken, I felt that who I am is not important. I thought I must be a stupid woman, that is why I made such a bad choice. I was left abandoned again, this time is in a whole new country which I knew nothing about and where I didn't even speak English.

I hated myself for many years. The hate kept me going with a constant voice in my head that I needed to be successful to prove I was not a loser. I needed to prove that constantly. I took any job I could find. I cleaned people's houses while I was going to ESL school, going to massage school and getting a driver's license, all the while focusing on taking care of my daughter.

Four years later, I started my own business. My business grew each year. I opened three spas and bought my house in Silicon Valley. Although my business was growing, the wounded heart and traumatic stress of fighting alone and pushing myself forward to stay strong to prove that I had value as a woman. I was exhausted and lonely. I could not feel happy. It seemed I never did enough.

My overachieving came with traumatic stress and started to destroy my health.

A few months ago, in one week I called an ambulance twice. My blood pressure was 235. I had a panic attack. I felt my heart jump out of my chest. When I was lying there in an ambulance, I asked myself, "Think, think quick, Riya. If you die today, how will you have lived your life?

If you died today, what will be the meaning of your life? Does your life really matter?

That fifteen minutes trip to the hospital seemed like the longest ride I have had in my life. I knew I didn't want to live the way I had been living anymore. I knew I needed to change my life at that moment.

The Last Day At the Spa

Now I am sitting in my green chair at my beautiful spa. Today will be the last day of my stay in my spa. After I decided to change, I started to sell my house, my business, my car, everything I owned. I was now going to travel and to search for my happiness and the meaning of my life.

How would I find it? I did not know, I only knew I had to go. I would find it on the road.

I became a traveler on the road to discover my soul and to search for my own happiness.

Mysterious City of Sertar

I arrived in Sertar. It is my third time visiting Tibet in the past twenty years. But this is my first time in Sertar. A city with an elevation oof 4,127 m (13,540 ft) is a county in the northwest of Sichuan Province, China, and has the world's largest Tibetan Buddhist institute.

It was day seven since I arrived here. I still can feel a slight headache. I know my headaches are from high elevation. Even though I had spent a month in the Tibetan mountains previously, I was slow to get used to the high elevations. As I looked through the windows, I saw it was raining outside. As the drizzle hits the rooftop, I can hear the sound of raindrops splashing. A few crows are jumping on the rooftop and flying around, enjoying the rain. My mind is still drifting from the images I saw yesterday. I had known about a ritual called a sky burial for a long time, but this was my first time so close to seeing it. The Sky burial is a funeral practice in which a human corpse is placed on a mountaintop to decompose while exposed to the elements and to be eaten by scavenging animals, especially carrion birds.

The majority of Tibetan people teach the transmigration of spirits.

"There is no need to preserve the body, as it is now an empty vessel. Birds may eat it, or nature may cause it to decompose. The function of the sky burial is simply to dispose of the remains in as generous of a way as possible. (The origin of the practice's Tibetan name.)

That day I witnessed seven bodies fed to vultures my mind was shocked. I could have never imagined it if I was not there. It prompted many thoughts about my own life and my own death. What would I want to do with my body when I die?

I spent three months in different Tibetan villages. Visited a different Tibetan monasteries. I stayed in the monastery to study chanting, meditation, and Tibetan healing methods.

After Tibet, I went to Nepal, a small country on the other side of Himalayan mountains. On my birthday that year in Nepal, I gave a birthday gift to myself of going to a small village and signing up for a ten day silent meditation course.

In those ten days of silence, the rule was no exercise, no writing, no nothing. Each day we started sitting meditation at 4:30 a.m. and went till 9:00 p.m. My body and my emotions were like a roller coaster up and down. The physical pain from long sitting brought out all my emotions: sadness, anger, fear, guilt.

Trillions of thoughts flow through my mind each day, and each day there was a bit shift, changes and evolving. I went from fighting my thoughts to become more observant of them. With each day's meditation, slowly I became more connected to my heart. My painful thoughts and struggles became less and less. The gratitude and love started rising in my heart. I realized I did have people who loved me: my father, my daughter, my friends, even my mom. They just all have their own way of showing their love to me. It's me who never learned how to love myself. During the meditation, as I start to recognize it, my mind shifted, and even my body started vibrating and feeling lighter. The gratitude, love, and compassion started racing in in my heart.

I see the light!

There is a door behind the darkness. The light is always there, paralleled behind the door. I was blinded by my fear. When I overcome the fear, the doors are opened, the lights light up my heart.

On my last day of meditation, I suddenly felt and saw a beautiful lotus flower rising from my heart to my third eye and blooming inside me. At that moment I forget who I was and where I was at. I just felt that I was the lotus and the lotus was me.

During the past two and half years, I have traveled to more than thirty countries and over a hundred cities. I did a lot of self-healing and a lot of meditation. I created a lot of changes in my life. Some were scary, some were joyful. I have been through a lot of struggles, loneliness, and tears. I have also brought a lot of love, laughter, joy and blessings. Throughout the waves of changes, one thing has really stood out. It's okay to be scared and to be vulnerable, but it is also OK to be bold, courageous, and curious in life. I finally feel whole, standing in my true self, and growing to love myself. I am finally falling in love with myself! My love to my inner self gives me the confidence to expand my manifesting power. I know it's not that I caught a lucky break. I am not more special than anyone else. In truth, I am just all in with my self-healing, self-love, commitment and my desire for change. I am all in, throwing myself out there to ride the waves of my self-healing journey. I continue step by step on my self-healing journey, I gather knowledge, experience, and strength to manifest a life I love.

Once, one of my clients asked me, "Riya, what's your meaning of falling in love with yourself? What does that feel like? Each time I see you, I can feel your joy and passion vibrate throughout your energy. I want to be like that too. What can I do to become in love with myself as well?"

I smiled to her and said: "Falling in love with myself is not just feelings. It's an action, it's a vibration, it's an energy. Each morning I wake up and feel fresh, love, gratitude and passion. I am no longer looking for someone or something to bring happiness to me, because I already have it inside me."

Be bold. Be curious. Be your true self.

From my own healing journey I found the meaning of my life, my purpose, and my passion. That is to infuse a spiritual practice into my daily life, both personal and professional, for an elevated living experience and to live a fulfilled and joyful life. At the same time I aspire to serve and help others.

If part of my story inspires you and you feel a deep yearning for something in your own life to change, consider to asking yourself these questions:

1. Do you trust your intuition?

2. Do you have difficulty concentrating?

3. Do you constantly justify and give reasons for acting without love?

4. Do you know who you truly are? What's your deepest desire?

5. What is your superpower?

6. How do you like being you?

If you have the answers or want to find those answers, please reach out to me. I would love to hear from you and we can discover these questions together.

Book a discovery call with me: https://calendly.com/riyawang/free-consultation

Here is a link to the free gift of "Emotional Freedom Worksheet":

https://www.zenquency-artofhealing.com/free-gift

Riya Wang

I am Riya Wang, a transformational healer and a visionary spiritual coach who guides people to align with their true callings and find inner peace. It is my soul mission to help you tap into your birthright of a fulfilled and joyful life.

I am well-traveled and bring diverse, life-changing healing techniques directly from my masters from around the world. My methods include self-reflection, self-awareness, transcendence, body, mind, and soul alignment. I also use additional techniques for transformative healing and a deepening of the practice of inner knowing. I also conduct and lead numerous meditation classes, sound healing workshops, transformational courses, and individual healing sessions.

I am passionate about helping others infuse a spiritual mindset into their daily lives, personal or professional, for an elevated living experience.

Riya Wang
Certificate, Chopra life coach
Certificate, Chopra meditation teacher
Certificate, state of California, sound healing therapy
Tibetan singing bowl teacher
Transformational Healing mentor
Visionary business coach
Email:
riyawang369@gmail.com
Website:
https://www.zenquency-artofhealing.com
Facebook:
Zenquency Healing Vibration,
https://www.facebook.com/groups/569953247232397
LinkedIn:
Riya (Rebecca) Wang,
https://www.linkedin.com/in/riya-wang-7933a327/

YouTube:
Zenquency Art of Healing,
https://www.youtube.com/channel/UCBF0pT3vNVuA0f62Eq35Rdg
Instagram:
Zenquency Art of Healing,
https://instagram.com/zenquency_artofhealing

FROM CAREGIVER TO CEO
BY HELEN MILLER-MONTANA

"If you want the moon, do not hide from the night. If you want a rose, do not run away from the thorns."
—Rumi

Life can change from one moment to the next and present a frightening new reality when a loved one "kisses the other side." When I decided to write this chapter, my intention was to share how my family and I survived a massive stroke, even triumphed, in hopes to provide insights, best practices, and resources to others going through the same journey of caregiving.

Mine was a childhood that took me from the Netherlands to Madrid where I was born and spent my wee years; eventually to Kansas, where my father accepted a job with Boeing; and, at seventeen, running off to join the Army and, not long after, meeting the love of my life, Bert. After finishing Basic Training at Fort Jackson, South Carolina, and AIT (Advanced Individual Training) for M36 MOS as Chaplain Assistant at the Chaplain Training School at Fort Monmouth, New Jersey, I returned home to Kansas, where I packed up the farming wagon for a vacation to California.

Within nine days of arriving to the Bay Area, I was hired at an insurance brokerage firm in Palo Alto. With this opportunity, I knew the vacation was over and I would never return to Kansas. California offered so much, and I loved the diversity, high energy, and fast pace of Silicon Valley! I also loved the brilliant, innovative minds of the people from which I got to meet, learn and work. The nightclub scene was far more thrilling, edgy, and imaginative, too! Discoveries abounded in my first few months, and soon after, I met the love of my life! Observing him from afar, striding across the lawn at my apartment complex with a virile confidence that caught my breath, akin to love at first sight, though I had not yet seen the beauty of his face. It wasn't until a few days later, as I parked and opened the wagon's back passenger door, my grocery bags spilled out onto the carport cement floor. I scrambled to catch the rolling cans and fruit as someone walked past. I was bent down trying to quickly fill the bags when I heard a lovely deep voice say, "Do you need any help?" Startled, I looked up to find my gorgeous Bert and said, "Sure. Thank you." He helped fill the bags and followed me to my apartment. He carried a full bag in a way I had never seen, on the palm of his hand as if it was an empty tray, and I was able to see the fine development of his muscular arms. From that day, Bert swept me off my feet and spoiled me beyond imagination. He became my superhero whose love was staggering and simply blew my mind. Bert taught me how to weight-train, encouraged me to pursue higher education, and supported my career dreams. He remodeled lovely homes for us, traveled abroad though apprehensive because he knew I loved to, and I knew at any moment throughout the day, he was thinking of me. The next twenty-eight years were pure bliss, fantastical, productive, adventurous, filled with new experiences, and I viewed the world through rose-colored glasses.

Bert grew in his career in construction after giving up a law-enforcement path. From hanging drywall, he eventually became a general contractor launching his own business, Big Sky Construction, where he built a loyal clientele and grew his business. My career journey led me to Apple as a project coordinator, accountant, and eventually supporting the controller as his assistant in headquarters. Eventually, I joined engineers launching a startup which led to having been a part of three M&As and one IPO. Bert and I loved the work we both did and continued relishing in our mad love affair. Life was beautiful each day, and the thought of our future was exciting!

I launched the Dell Silicon Valley Toastmasters Club for our engineers to develop presentation skills, as many had interest in applying for leadership positions at our acquiring company. I was scheduled to attend an event the evening of April 10, 2013. Unexpectedly and intuitively, I felt the need to stay home and finish office work. I struggled with this decision, as this was an important event. As I worked in my home office, I heard a crash in the living room and called out, "Bert, is everything okay?" After not hearing anything, I ran to the living room, seeing him on the floor between the couch and ottoman with eyes that looked happy to see me, but no sound from him nor the ability to lift himself from one side of his body. I immediately picked up our puppy, Rocco, and ran to my office to grab my cell phone and leave the puppy behind closed doors because I knew there was something serious looming before us. While on the floor with Bert, I immediately called our friend and nurse, Chris, who ran across the street in a couple of minutes with his medical bag. He immediately directed me to call 911 upon seeing Bert's inability to speak or move the right side of his body. Within minutes, the ambulance arrived and took Bert to the hospital. Chris and I followed. Bert made it to ER within twenty-four minutes from when I found him. They administered the clot-busting medication—tissue plasminogen activator (tPA)—to break up the blood clot in his brain. Bert was diagnosed as having had a massive ischemic stroke in his left carotid artery, and from that moment, life as we knew it was no more.

For the next nine days, Bert spent a volatile stay in ICU/CCU, where his heart was erratic for the first six days until they realized he didn't need dopamine. When Bert and I returned home after nearly a month in the hospital and rehabilitation, it was like a new experience for him as his memory was affected and he was having to learn things again. We moved slowly to help him acclimate back home. He had sustained six percent brain injury, which left him without memories of our home, our relationship or me. It would be three years later that I would learn that my sweet Bert would express that he didn't know me and couldn't remember our relationship before the event of his stroke. Those blissful many years together are gone for him.

We took the next several months slowly, lots of tenderness, many naps, much quiet time after his therapies at home with three wonderful therapists visiting for an hour at a time for occupational, speech, and physical therapy. After good progress and with the approval from his physical therapist, I reintroduced him to weight training at Gold's Gym. Bert was also running on the Campbell track. He was amazing, and his doctors stated that Bert's athleticism all of his life helped his muscle memory return quickly. Dr. Wolfe, a neurointerventionist, suspected Bert had unknowingly injured his left carotid artery during his wrestling days which built up scar tissue and plaque and eventually closed, causing the stroke. The greatest challenge has been and currently is speech, as Bert's brain was greatly affected in the Wernicke area of the left hemisphere as well as part of the prefrontal cortex.

After stabilizing Bert's medical condition to a great extent, I slowly introduced him to activities such as board games, social time with small gatherings at our home for lunch with our closest family and friends, car rides to areas that he used to know, and eventually learning how to drive again, starting with empty parking lots, then graduating to country roads and eventually around our neighborhood, where today he is once again a better driver than me. We spent much time with his neurologist, cardiologist, primary care physician, vascular surgeon, and other medical care providers. I also experimented with other types of healing, such as acupuncture, hyperbaric oxygen treatment, and massage.

As Bert's construction business clients waited for him to recover, we slowly began taking on small projects such as painting, building a fence, and door replacements. I stayed with Bert on the job sites and had one of his foremen work closely with Bert as he was introduced to simple tasks. After a few months, Bert shared that he didn't want to continue, and so we transitioned all of his clients over to his two foremen and gave them Bert's construction business as they had families of their own to support.

The first four years of Bert's stroke, I was intently focused on Bert's recovery, seeking medical expertise, improving Bert's aphasic condition, ensuring his daily contentment to prevent depression, administering his daily medications, introducing activities to improve his quality of life, and managing his medicine-induced impulsive outbursts which required controlling and restraining his physical attacks. These became more and more frightening and were most heart-breaking for me to see him in this state of rage as this was not who Bert was before the stroke.

As we continued meeting with doctors and specialists to resolve issues, I began recognizing medical professionals are not infallible. They too have families that need them, they have their own ailments, they are stretched with many patients, and they can make mistakes. This is when I began noticing that it was not unusual for a medical professional to forget which patient or case they were treating. Who is Bert? What was his last condition? Why did he receive another prescription? Why does he have to continue it? I wasn't getting satisfactory responses when I began learning more about these medications and questioning their value. When I began receiving responses that were rhetoric, I knew I had to learn more, and so

I did. Bert was taking ten medications at the onset of stroke. After years of partnering with Bert's doctors through daily recordings, tracking data, discussing treatments, reasoning for medication reduction, today Bert is down to two medications and living a "new normal" quality of life where he has regained a level of confidence, is largely independent, able to think critically, contribute to our home, and rebuild a life together again.

By the second year of being a full-time caregiver, I needed to generate income for our household if I wanted to maintain our lifestyle and remain in Silicon Valley. So, I started my plan to launch my business where I could work predominantly from home and simultaneously care for Bert. I built up my network, connecting to startup leaders on LinkedIn. I would sit next to Bert (on his right side to help him regain his peripheral vision) on the sofa while he watched basketball. I refined my profile to serve those that would eventually become my clients. It was at this time that I reached out to my former startup CEOs, informing them that I was launching and needed their help. I am so grateful for their guidance, support, and patronage as it was with their help that VentureOps was launched (and named by a former CEO). I began my service supporting early-stage technical startups, offering HR, finance, payroll, administrative, and facilities management services. As more clients were signing on for service, I decided to offer the opportunity for other women to learn, work, and benefit from the technical startup industry, which has been predominantly male led and operated. With this goal in mind, I began hiring and training women on startup operations and placing them in the tech startups. As each woman had an area of specialty, we cross-trained for the various functions. Our team consisted of women who were single mothers, women who needed to supplement their income, women who wanted to rejoin the workforce after taking time off to raise their families, and disabled and elder women able to provide a service working from home. As I began building a team, I too was learning new skills and became a full-fledged staffing agent for my clients. I was involved with recruiting not only administrative and operational type candidates, but also began partnering with clients to staff their technical teams, establishing the process, organizing and tracking slews of candidate resumes, advising on contingent recruiter terms, and overseeing their service. Additionally, we scheduled innumerable candidate interviews as client startups ramped up, and we created in-house procedures for hiring leaders to follow. Business was picking up, and we built a team of six supporting our clients, not to include those whom we placed full-time as hired employees. I became creative in finding the perfect talent and serving our clients with very specific talent tailored to their needs, leadership personality, and company culture. As relationships are at the top of my strengths, I put a great deal in matchmaking for talent and companies. Those we have placed are win-win-win cases. My confidence soared as results were happy clients and happy placements and hires.

It was wonderful being able to connect with others who shared my passion for business and to have innovative, thought-provoking conversations. These interactions are easy to lose when in isolation as a caregiver.

As a caregiver, certain aspects of how I engaged with people heightened my ability to develop close and trusting relationships within my business. Empathy became a far more developed trait through caregiving, which transferred to how I was able to deeply understand the pain points of my clients, resolving and even anticipating to fix before they ever experienced the problem.

These newly developed skills translated to my business by way of fully offering support with a "servant's heart" and grateful mindset for having their trust and the opportunity to work with them. Additional leadership skills and strengths I further developed from being a caregiver showed up in my business in various ways.

When I think about how caregivers support their loved ones, it is easy to recognize the leadership skills they build and how these transferrable skills can build a business. It gives me great pleasure to share these most notable caregiving best practices, insights and skills that have been instrumental in my career and business.

Best practices and transferrable skills from caregiving to leadership:

1. **Lead with empathy.** To care for another with compassion, love and kindness, one must be able to put oneself in their loved one's place after they have suffered a serious health crisis. Dr. Jill Bolte Taylor's book *My Stroke of Insight* helped me understand Bert's stroke condition. He was wounded, unable to express himself and function normally. Dr. Bolte Taylor felt she returned to one hundred percent (though not exactly the same person) after her eighth year of having had her stroke. In retrospect, she needed others to treat her lovingly, encourage her, and find her as she was trapped deep within her injured brain. The team I have built all share in having a servant's heart when we work for our clients. We put our customers first and use empathy in how we serve them. Putting ourselves in

their shoes to be sure to provide the best support possible, even anticipating their needs, allows them to focus on their strategy, technology, and business at hand.

2. **Live in gratitude. Lead with integrity.** "Acknowledging the good that you already have in your life is the foundation for all abundance," as shared by Eckhart Tolle, helped me to have this mindset as a caregiver. Be grateful for each day, and smell the roses along the way. There will always be good and not-so-good days. To slow down to appreciate and savor the beauty around us is fulfilling. Living in gratitude and leading with optimism creates a harmonious, healing, and productive space for yourself and others. Count your blessings, hug your blessings, and be a blessing. In business, and especially as a business owner, you become an integral part of the financial circle of life. Get one, give one. Maya Angelou said, "When you learn, teach. When you get, give."

3. **Be patient; have tolerance and hope.** "Where there's hope, there's life. It fills us with fresh courage and makes us strong again." As Anne Frank wrote and lived by these precious words, it is for us to remember and emulate. With challenges of caregiving, I've expanded my ability to tolerate, to be patient, to pick my battles, to know when to let things go. As hard as it is to walk down an unknown path of this "new normal," taking one step at a time, slow and steady, helped me during this most difficult time. When Bert had the ischemic stroke which his doctors labeled massive, I braced for this challenge, committed with tremendous hope that I could bring my dearest husband back to his full identity and every attribute that made him uniquely Bert. Keeping expectations fluid, practicing patience, tolerance and humility is a daily necessity . . . and no doubt a fraction of Bert's practice of these standards. In business, there will be times that things don't go as planned, or others don't share your perspective, and when tough decisions must be made. It is during these times, practicing patience and tolerance while retaining hope helps get you through it.

4. **Accept change, be flexible, and adapt.** Accepting change in my home life as a caregiver was not easy. Once I did, I was able to progress in resolving each issue as it arose. I was far more effective when I focused more on solving a problem and less focused on the stress of change. This developed my ability in how I approached problem-solving in business. I became creative and agile in services

offered, developing solutions with customizable aspects specific to each customer, and recognizing that needs of the customer change with the digital transformation the technical industry is facing. Test out ideas, try new things, fail, and fail fast... iterate, iterate, iterate. Know that your first plan may not be your end plan, so be flexible in your business. Follow the market and work with your clients to understand their biggest pain points. Use the SDBS (Sell, Design, Build, Sell) method that was created by one of my mentors. As you have a concept, work with your potential customers understanding their greatest needs, collaborate with them on the solution, then build from that design. Once you have built and sold to them, you can offer to other clients with adjustments for them as needed. Be fluid in your service as it makes sense.

5. **Advocate, protect, and shield.** As your loved one is voiceless and vulnerable in every way, your role as a caregiver is to ensure their best interest is always served. Speak for your loved one who is unable to speak for him/herself. Always have someone with your loved one in the hospital to observe, to monitor, and raise awareness for aspects of your loved one's condition, situation, preferences, and threats that may not be apparent to someone that doesn't know him/her. As I partnered with the doctors, nurses and medical professionals, I became an extension of their service as I was happy to assist in caring for Bert. Caregivers are the voice for the powerless. Our advocacy saves lives. In business, our advocacy, protection, and shielding our teams allows them to do their best work and ultimately serve the business optimally.

6. **Celebrate wins.** Even celebrate the little ones. With Bert's aphasia, which keeps him from communicating fully, we gave high-fives for every new word he could say. We recognize accomplishments and tasks completed with a favorite meal, positive affirmation, and cheers with a toast at the dinner table. There are many ways to celebrate wins both at home and on the job. The point is to simply recognize and reward, whether in simple ways or with grand gestures. Even a sincere "thank you" can mean a lot at home and in business. Maya Angelou's words, "I've learned that people will forget what you said, what you did, but they will not forget how you made them feel," supports the idea to be acknowledged, respected, and celebrated are those memories that last a lifetime.

7. **Be bold and curious.** Ask for help, delegate, and know your opinions are important and can be the difference between life and death. Trust your gut, know yourself, listen to your intuition and follow your inspiration—it's there for a reason. Keep learning, and don't be afraid to question matters relating to medical treatment, medication, side effects, and service, and explore ideas, resources, health practices, etc. Bert has suffered from multiple medication inaccuracies that could have been much worse had these not been immediately identified. Don't expect perfection from anyone. In business, continue learning, and take opportunities that are new. As a leader, provide opportunities for learning to your employees. Make time for career development, personal growth, and strengthening skills for yourself and others.

8. **You are not alone,** though you may feel that way sometimes, especially in the beginning when you're trying to figure things out. Find your tribe and support from those in your life, and know they will come in and out of your life. Who you have today in your circle may not be who you have in the future, and that is okay. Open yourself to all potential relationships. Your interests will change, as will your opportunities. Join associations that align with your values. Be selective with your precious time and only allow positivity, optimism, and supportive, kind, loving people into your space (physically and mentally).

9. **Mentor and have coaches.** As a caregiver, ask for help and guidance from doctors, nurses and other medical professionals. Also ask for help, and appoint others to take on those matters that can be delegated. Invest time in networking, and seek the advice, guidance, and support of coaches, mentors, advocates, and sponsors. Remember to reciprocate as you can when they might have a need for help. Anticipate and be generous to them as they are with you.

10. **Self-care and balance.** Self-care is not selfish, and it is not a luxury. It simply is a necessity. Without you, what would become of your loved one? Take time to do things you love, spend time on your health—physically, mentally, emotionally and spiritually. Self-care can be tricky, especially in the beginning. It's better to plan your time for you instead of running out of steam to the point of your own decline. You are important, and for your loved one, especially important. Without your own health, physical, mental and emotional, you will not be able to help others. It's like the oxygen mask—put yours

on first. My "me time" is Sunday for four to five glorious hours! Bert allows me this time for just me. He sees how happy it makes me. I sleep in while he watches the news and has his fruit, then we watch a spiritual program together and have a simple breakfast of bagel breakfast sandwiches and coffee delivered to our front door. No cooking for me on Sunday morning. While Bert gardens and tinkers around the garage, I indulge for a couple of hours watching inspirational programs that help me restore, regenerate, create, and innovate. I keep this time sacred . . . just for me. Find time just for you. In business, it is important for leaders to model self-care for their teams, create effective ways for their employees to take care of themselves, and support work/life balance for self and others. To recruit and retain top talent is essential, and offering balance in work and life contributes to an employee's happiness at work.

11. **Have fun; be kind and optimistic.** Though life was especially scary when Bert first returned home from the hospital, it was important that his confusion, stress, and any anxiety were kept at minimum. I kept things light and easy. If he made a mistake, I would make a mistake, and we would laugh. Creating a fun, happy, and encouraging home from the start for Bert has been instrumental in gaining his trust, sense of security, building his confidence and ultimate success. This set the culture for my business and how I worked with my team and our customers. As the business grew, I slowly became aware of the type of clients I was willing to serve. I set the standard for me, the team, and with the same expectation for our clients as well. We spend many hours working, and these hours should be as pleasurable and positive as possible. The energy that surrounds us is critical for our wellness and ability to thrive.

If my story and lessons have resonated with and inspired you, I wholeheartedly invite you to join my Caregiving Tribe to meet and connect with others experiencing the same journey as a caregiver and provider. To offer a safe haven of support, story-sharing, collective empowerment, and a place where you are welcomed, cherished and feel connection with our tribe is my ultimate goal. I would also be pleased to share a report I have created with resources, contacts, and strategies, as well as hear back from you to know how these are working for you. With heartfelt gratitude, thank you for all you do for your loved ones and for taking this precious time to let me share my journey with you.

Helen Miller-Montana

Hello, my name is Helen Miller-Montana, and I have been in HR for fifteen years, serving Silicon Valley technology companies in both the private and public sectors. I am passionate about building lasting relationships and working within innovative technology environments. I am committed to fostering collaborative, transparent, and inclusive organizations. I provide people solutions in partnership with leaders to form strong teams, develop and empower employees to reach their full potential as well as create thriving corporate cultures.

I love spending time with my husband, Bert, and our little pup, Rocco, who brightens our day; gardening; and hanging out with my amazing sisters. I aspire to be creative and surround myself with beauty. My claim to fame is having danced "The Twist" with Chubby Checker when I was a young teen.

CaregiversTribe.com
Email: hello@caregiverstribe.com

EMPOWERED RECOVERY AND THE DANCE OF LIFE
BY CATHLENE MICHAELS-BRADER AND MATTHEW NOONAN

Have you ever been suffering to the point where you're ready to give up on life completely? Well, I was there about a year ago.

Since my twenty-fifth birthday, I had this overwhelming knowing that when I turned fifty, everything was going to change in my life. Just prior to my fiftieth birthday, I spent two weeks in an outpatient substance abuse program. Although I got some benefit, I knew it was not the change I was looking for. I turned fifty; I didn't have some miraculous epiphany of what I needed to do next in order to shift my life. Once again, I was spiraling down into depression.

I knew that the amount of substance I was using and the amount of alcohol I was drinking was killing me. The physical and emotional pain was constant, causing my rage to bubble constantly to the surface. I could be easily triggered by anything and anyone. I was even afraid of myself.

About five days after my birthday, I received a text from Cathlene wishing me a happy birthday. Instead of texting, I simply pushed the dial button. When she answered, I said, "I think you can help me."

When we decided to contribute our story to the Awakened Leaders project, we sat down with our mentor and talked to her about how our work as facilitators of healing impacts the lives of others. The following is the conversation we had.

Cathlene, what did you think when Matthew called?

When I saw Matthew's name on the phone, I was elated. For the first time since we met almost three years ago, here was an actual call from Matthew. There was one exception: he surprised me with an invitation to dinner on one of his visits to town. That dinner lasted over four hours; then he disappeared again. Most people would have given up. Some of my friends said I should. However, when we met in that fateful class, I instantly knew that Matthew was my soulmate.

How did you know that Matthew was your soulmate?

It felt like a lightning bolt realigning my chakras along with every cell in my body. There was a clicking mechanism in the background, like a key opening a door to a chamber in my heart that I didn't even know was there until I met Matthew. It was not like any other sense of coming together with another being that I've ever experienced in my life.

Matthew, did you have a reaction to Cathlene when you first met?

I felt an energetic connection that I had no idea what to do with. It actually terrified me. I was already in a constant state of overwhelm, which was only modulated by using substances. What I find interesting now is that I thought I was only drawn to Sequim, Washington, because of the spiritual work I was doing, but in actuality I was drawn to Sequim, Washington, by Cathlene.

Cathlene, when Matthew called, what other feelings were you having?

I think it is important to share with you what I was feeling before the phone call. About two months before the phone call, I was in a place of longing, you know, the type of longing that hurts in your heart for "the one." This was odd for me because I follow a philosophy which says that there is a place in our being where we can be whole and complete within ourselves.

One time when I was driving, the longing was so intense that I stopped the car to scream at the universe, "If you don't want me to have longing, then you better damn well fill me up right now." I got the biggest surprise of my life because the universe filled me up with love.

What did that feel like?

It felt like a warm sensation coming up from the bottom of my feet all the way up to the top of my head. I was so full of love, compassion, and quiet. There was no longing or lack. It allowed me to move forward in an easier way without suffering. I continued to work on myself. This was ultimately a two-year process of delving into how I love people and the expectations I still had about relationships. I utilized my thirty-plus years of knowledge as a Holistic Health Practitioner—on myself. To finally answer your question about how I was feeling when Matthew called, I was actually in a neutral place but very happy that he called.

What was your response when Matthew said, "I think you can help me"?

"What do you want me to help you with?" Matthew explained, "I need you to help me come off drugs and alcohol." I knew I could help him because of the extensive knowledge I have in complementary medicine. However, what was important to consider was that boundaries needed to be established in certain areas. I was also hoping we would have a more intimate relationship in time, so boundaries were necessary.

I told him, "I can help you with several areas. The areas we can start with are clearing, nutrition, and herbal remedies, and I can be there for you through your process. I can't be your counselor, so when we get to the place where you need to have a counselor, we will get you one."

How long did you talk that day?

I believe we talked for at least eight hours. It was amazing. It felt like the universe was definitely helping to keep that connection, because neither one of our phones died during that entire conversation.

What happened after that phone call?

We talked on the phone every waking moment. We got to know each other, starting to really create a rapport. We began doing clearing work, releasing programs, beliefs, and patterns that limited Matthew's ability to express his authentic self.

How do you clear programs, beliefs and patterns?

Using muscle testing to determine where the limitations are located, we can decide which method or technique will be used to clear that limitation. There are clearing processes that you can do to help shift patterns out of your life. The first thing we do is find out if the pattern is mental, emotional, physical, or spiritual.

How was it for you, Matthew?

The level of trust that we created so quickly became the most amazing experience I've ever had. My mind was being opened to concepts that I had no idea were even possible. The fact that you can clear limiting patterns and programs from your life is amazing. Up until this time, I felt like a victim of the anxiety I carried my entire life.

With each clearing, I gained another level of calm. I got excited about the possibility that there would be a way for me to actually come off of substance. I saw light at the end of the tunnel. For the first time, I had hope.

Did you also see a relationship?

Yes, the two seem to go hand in hand. The more that I was learning, the more my heart opened up to Cathlene.

Did you see a relationship forming, Cathlene?

Yes, for the first time I was able to talk to a man and really say anything, explore anything with him. I've never encountered a man in my life where I could actually do that, not even my late husband. It was very freeing.

Matthew, do you think Cathlene was pushing you to change?

No, not at all. The desire to stop using substances was really completely on my end. I felt that she was there to support me in every way. I never felt a push from Cathlene or any judgment from her. She truly accepted me as I was. This was the key to my being able to move forward.

What made you stop going to recovery programs?

Most treatment centers require you to be sober when entering their programs. Without removing the triggers or causes that made me want to get high, how do I get sober? This never made any sense to me. I needed help to get sober.

One of the most significant things about being in recovery with Cathlene was that she didn't vilify substance or the person using. We did not substitute one addiction for another; we started discovering the reasons why I needed drugs and alcohol to get through life. I was using substance as a coping mechanism.

What have you discovered since you started delving deeper into your recovery process?

I found that during this year when you don't use resistance to change a habit, what happens is you witness your desire. When you don't squelch that desire, you can examine it. Then you ask why you have the desire in the first place. I know now that this is the only way I can have any peace of mind, any peace in life. As we began to explore my memories and experiences, I found that these were the things I was trying to push down. As each new revelation came up, we would either clear it or remove it from my atomic structure instead of resisting it.

I did not quit substance use cold turkey; Cathlene left that up to me to decide. This was very empowering. I decided when, where, and how to stop using substances. First, I stopped using methamphetamine. After about three months of clearing, taking supplements, and changes to my diet, I was able to stop the drinking. Finally, nine months after that, I had learned enough healthy coping mechanisms to be able to release the use of marijuana and CBD. We all live life, and I still get triggered now and then to have a drink or smoke marijuana, but I have enough empowerment, which leaves me in a conscious state, so that I can release the thought and not be a victim of those urges.

Cathlene, how has Matthew's process affected you?

By being in this relationship, I've shed many patterns of my own. I have no doubt that we are in the process of becoming equal partners. The year of Matthew being in recovery has been an education for me as well as for him.

Matthew, when did you start talking to a counselor?

Shortly after I started living with Cathlene.

I really understood the need to have a third-party counselor. If you're really baring your soul and finding what your challenges are, you need somebody who is willing to not pull punches.

Cathlene, why did you think a counselor was needed?

The main reason to talk to a counselor is that it prevents the creation of the "power over" dynamic in a relationship. This is where one in the relationship is always less than the other and neither partner can emerge in their wholeness.

Matthew, where do think you are in the recovery process right now?

I am completely off of any mood-altering substances at this time and gaining more clarity daily than I ever knew was possible. As of yesterday, I realized that I want to live.

What changed your mind about living?

I recognized the real work and the real purpose for me being here. The truth is I can bring my higher self into this physical body. The discovery of this truth has re-energized me and given me a reason to want to live.

How does that make you feel, Cathlene?

When Matthew told me he wanted to live, I cried in joy! All of the things that we have been doing in the last year have really allowed him to come to this point. I am happy that the steps we took with herbs, clearings, and other therapies empowered him to shift on a physical level so he could focus on his spiritual journey.

Say more about how this journey is for you, Matthew.

In the process of becoming an awakened leader, it has given me a good foundation to step out on my own and stand in my power. I can see all of my previous experiences with clarity and see how they actually were a necessary part of my life. They no longer trigger me because we've cleared away the shame, guilt, and rage that came up with each memory. I'm just beginning to see the benefits of my life experience now.

Cathlene and Matthew, are you now on the same page with each other?

We are.

What is a relationship to you, Cathlene?

For me it is open, honest, loving communication of two people standing side by side, not only witnessing each other's lives but participating in them.

How do you feel about that definition, Matthew?

Oh, I agree with it. Our relationship changes and evolves every day. Our love and the level of intimacy we share grows deeper in ways I didn't even know were possible. We are willing to question and explore ourselves individually and then bring it to each other with trust that the other will truly listen. Even if one or the other gets triggered by what is being said, we can walk through the issues knowing that we have honesty in our relationship to get us through it.

I now know this is the type of relationship I have always wanted but didn't know that it takes two to do the dance.

How does it feel to be in the dance of your relationship?

We see the dance as being able to walk this path, exploring and delving into thought patterns, actions, behaviors, and occurrences, finding out which ones are ours and which are not. All of the ones that are not ours and not for our highest good, we clear out of our pathway so we can step into life, as all of who we are.

We have found in our own coming together that we were initially working around and with the programs that we each were running. But we stopped, acknowledged the patterns or programs, then cleared them so that they no longer interfered with the dance of our relationship.

The other dance that has been created by us coming together is that Matthew and I are now working seamlessly together in our healing practice. We are standing side by side in flow creating a life together.

Now that the conversation we had with our mentor is finished, if you would like to explore the dance of life and begin to clear your own pathway, we invite you to take the journey with us.

Please feel free to contact us via e-mail at: cmlotus@sbcglobal.net or matthewstevennoonan@gmail.com

Cathlene Michaels-Brader and Matthew Noonan

Cathlene Michaels-Brader, BS, CHHPE, has a Bachelor of Science degree and is a certified holistic health practitioner and educator. She has had careers as an herbal formulator and a custom aromatherapy blend creator. Cathlene specializes in helping people identify and release patterns and beliefs in themselves that they no longer wish to express in their lives. During her thirty-plus years working in the health and wellness industry, she has explored how to bring science and spirit together to work synergistically.

Matthew Steven Noonan is a Reiki master and certified theta practitioner. He is a naturally gifted healer. With Matthew's abilities as an intuitive healer and empath, he has been helping people throughout his life on many levels. He is continually working to live a conscious life and is committed to helping others do the same.

Cathlene and Matthew have come together, combining their life experience and education to help themselves and others release the limitations that may keep us all from being our authentic selves.

Please contact us via e-mail at: cmlotus@sbcglobal.net or matthewstevennoonan@gmail.com

CLOSING THOUGHTS

We hope you have enjoyed your journey through these inspiring stories of self-healing, triumph and transformation by these Awakened Leaders. It is our hope that you will be inspired to share your own self-healing journey back to your soul's divine essence and powerful purpose in order to live your best life in a beautiful and peaceful world.

If this book has inspired you, we would love to hear from you! Please don't keep it to yourself. Give it as a gift to someone you love or share a few kind words in social media to help us raise awareness of our Awakened Leaders book project and our objective to empower the planet.

Please be sure subscribe to the BodyMindSoul.TV & media network to get all the latest Positive Vibes with Aeriol and Chakra Tone Rx episodes and receive ongoing information about upcoming books, livestream events or self-healing classes.

Please use the QR Code Below to view each author speaking about their chapter in our Awakened Leaders Book Talk Series:

REVIEWS

"*Awakened Leaders* inspires us all to step more fully into our gifts, stretch our leadership wings, awaken to our full potential and SHINE! The tips, insights, and deep wisdom will empower you to embrace your full leadership potential."
—**Rebecca Hall Gruyter**, Empowerment Leader and CEO of RHG Media Productions
www.YourPurposeDrivenPractice.com

"*Awakened Leaders* is a timely read for anyone heeding the calling of their soul to wake up and reclaim their rightful place on earth. This collection from high powered, heart and soul centered leaders, is certain to help shift the consciousness of our planet through their stories, insights and wisdom."
—**Wendy Lee Baldwin Hargett**, Personal Growth Mentor, www.alignwithjoy.com

"This book has something for everyone. The stories featured in *Awakened Leaders: Empowering Stories of Self-Healing, Triumph and Transformation* speak to anyone seeking growth and understanding on their own self-healing path. The pages are filled with honesty and inspiration as Aeriol and her co-authors share their unique and personal journeys. And it's quite possible you find similarities in your own experience--perhaps one that resonates with you in a way leading to further self-discovery and transformation. Readers will enjoy a blend of compelling stories infused with tips and techniques that elevates the soul for optimal healing and joyous living."
—**Heather Larkin**, KC Holistic Healing kcholistichealing.com

"Amongst a poignant collection of stories, Aeriol Ascher shares an inspiring spiritual experience through vivid words that anyone on a soul journey can relate to. After reading, I found myself feeling encouraged, aware, and understood."
—**Shelby Kottemann**, International best selling Author, Inspirational Speaker, Reiki Master Healer shelbykottemann.com

"The three parts of *Awakened Leaders* are the symbols of a transformational process: a significant moment turns our world upside down causing torment, but at the same time, presenting us with a moment of enlightenment that leads us through the hardship, through the change, till we end up building a legacy. I can't but applaud the strength of the leaders who have unveiled their vulnerability and offered their stories for others to take inspiration, to uplift others going through a life-changing transformation. From spiritual self-healing to the transformative experience of building a family, to applying principles of caregiving in leadership, *Awakened Leaders* offers something relatable to each reader. Read and be inspired!"

—**Andrea Lewis,** Writer, Poet, Essayist, Co-author of *The Truth That Can't Be Told*
https://thetruththatcantbetold.com

"In our ever-changing world, practical, passionate, and professional leadership is paramount. Whether it's calling on Divine Feminine principles, discovering personal self-care options, providing compassionate caregiving for loved ones, or exploring how to best serve teams, the tools and techniques in this book will transform your life. Leadership comes in many forms. You'll glean tidbits in the heart-felt stories as these leaders guide you through the tunnel, lighting your way to the brighter world that awaits you."

—**Linda Lenore**, M.A. Feng Shui Master, award-winning speaker and author of *The Gift of the Red Envelope*
www.LindaLenore.com

"With a variety of authors openly telling their personal experiences and generously sharing the tactics and practices that served them; readers will no doubt find circumstances to which they can relate and guidance that will help them find peace, love themselves and powerfully leave their special mark on our world."

—**Amy Riley,** The Courage of a Leader Keynote Speaker, #1 International Best Selling Author, Consultant and Coach
www.courageofaleader.com

"These awakened leaders share their vulnerable stories through their strength and courage in order to achieve their triumphant success, personally and professionally.
I am sure you will each relate to their personal stories that will also help transform you to rise like the phoenix and to stand in your power to make an impact on generations to come."

—**Linda Joy Benn**, Transformational Catalyst, Founder of the Benn Method™ https://lindabenn.com

"In a time calling for healing, *Awakened Leaders* is just what the doctor ordered. Aeriol Ascher brings forth another powerful book filled with joy, love and inspiration. Start your own healing journey today with *Awakened Leaders*."

—**Maureen Ryan Blake,** Founder of The Power of the Tribe https://thepoweroftthetribe.com

"These awakened leaders share their vulnerable stories through their strength and courage in order to achieve their triumphant success, personally and professionally.
I am sure you will each relate to their personal stories that will also help transform you to rise like the phoenix and to stand in your power to make an impact on generations to come."

—**Linda Joy Benn**, Transformational Catalyst, Founder of the Benn Method™ https://lindabenn.com

"*Awakened Leaders* is an amazing collection of stories that inspires you to break free and embrace your own leadership so that you can Shine Your Brilliance with your gifts."

—**Seema Giri**, Best Selling and Award-Winning Author, Speaker, Book Writing Mentor and Founder of Uplyft Media

ABOUT BODYMINDSOUL.TV NETWORK

The BodyMindSoul.TV & Media Network was created in order to be a portal and platform committed to supporting the voices of healing on the planet. I hope this book has not only supported you, as a leader to take a fresh perspective on your own journey but also inspired you to plot a course and take action to bring your own voice forward onto the global stage.

If you are wanting to reach more people and be part of healing and inspiring others with your story, your gifts, and the work that you bring to the world, then I want to share some opportunities for you to consider.

We compile and produce an anthology book projects (stay tuned for us to announce 2023 projects) to support healing on the planet as well as spotlight and support the co-author's as they bring their work forward. We also produce a live streaming online TV show, facilitate speaker conferences, and conduct feature podcast interviews, in other words, we help experts like yourself step powerfully into the spotlight from a position of influence so they can make a global difference.

We provide group programs and strategies to help you get your voice heard and get your healing work seen by our audience and affiliated networks. We would love to support you in reaching more people to raise awareness of your work and also to raise the consciousness of the planet. Please take a moment to learn a little bit more about at the sites listed below, and then reach out to us for a conversation. **We would love to help show up, speak up and stand out. Isn't it time the world heard your story?**

If you would like to connect with me personally to explore some of our opportunities in upcoming book projects, speaker success training, podcast production training, podcast interview opportunities, feature speaker spots on our summits, or one on one coaching then please reach out to schedule a time to speak with me directly.

Learn more about my work: **www.AeriolAscher.com**

Email: AskAeriol@AeriolAscher.com

May you always choose to Be Seen, Heard, and leave a legacy of love.

Happy Healing!

Warmly,

Aeriol Ascher

Aeriol Ascher

Aeriol Ascher, MsD. is a #1 international bestselling Author many times over. She is an award winning media producer and show host and the founder of the BodyMindSoul.TV & Media Network, the proud recipient of three Communicator Awards of Distinction from the Academy of Interactive Visual Arts for her Streaming TV Series and Podcast Interview Series

Aeriol's recent book compilation **Empowered Self-Care: Healing Body Mind and Soul for a Better World** became a best seller in 56 categories across 5 countries and 21 of those categories made it to the #1 position. It is Aeriol's personal mission is to raise the consciousness of the planet one soul at a time and she believes that by leading, producing and publishing holistic media and programs that educate, uplift and inspire self mastery she is doing her part.

As a Book Compiler, Speaking Coach and Empowerment Leader Aeriol has a passion for guiding heart centered entrepreneurs, practitioners, educators, and coaches to show up, speak up and stand out so they can embrace their authentic and soul aligned success.: www.AeriolAscher.com

AERIOL PUBLISHING

Aeriol Publishing: books compiled by Aeriol Ascher

(*available on Amazon or our website* www.aeriolascher.com *shop*)

- **Empowered Self-Care: Healing, Body, Mind and Soul for a better World** Anthology book compiled by Aeriol Ascher 2021 RHG Media Productions CA
- **Awakened Leaders: Empowering Stories of Self-Healing, Triumph and Transformation** Anthology book compiled by Acriol Ascher (April 2022)

Best Selling Anthology books featuring Author, Aeriol Ascher:

(*available on Amazon or on* www.aeriolascher.com *website shop*)

- **The Animal Legacies:** by Rebecca Hall Gruyter 2019 RHG Media Productions
- **Experts and Influencers: The Leadership Edition** by Rebecca Hall Gruyter, 2019, RHG Media Productions
- **Experts and Influencers: The Women's Empowerment Edition** Anthology compiled by Rebecca Hall Gruyter, 2020, RHG Media Productions
- **Experts and Influencers: Move Forward with Purpose Edition** Anthology compiled by Rebecca Hall Gruyter, 2021, RHG Media Productions

Aeriol Publishing: Self-Reflection Journals:

(available on Amazon or available on www.aeriolascher.com website shop)

- The Self-Mastery Journal: Awakening Divine Purpose
- The Self-Mastery Journal: Inner Vision and Clarity
- The Self-Mastery Journal: Authentic Truth and Leadership
- The Self-Mastery Journal: Self-Love and Forgiveness
- The Self-Mastery Journal: Emotional Wellness, Energy and Vitality
- The Self-Mastery Journal: Inspired Creation and Community
- The Self-Mastery Journal: Presence, Power and Passion

Other Journals featuring Author, Aeriol Ascher:

(available on Amazon or our available on www.aeriolascher.com website shop)

- The Animal Legacies Journal
- Experts and Influencers: Women's Empowerment Journal

Aeriol Publishing: Wisdom Oracle Card Decks

(available on www.aeriolascher.com website shop only)

- Empowered Self-Care Wisdom Cards
- Self-Mastery Oracle Cards

Other Wisdom Card Decks Featuring Author, Aeriol Ascher

(available on www.aeriolascher.com website shop only)

- The Animal Legacies Wisdom Card Deck
- Experts & Influencers: Women's Empowerment Wisdom Deck

www.ingramcontent.com/pod-product-compliance
Lightning Source LLC
LaVergne TN
LVHW010219070526
838199LV00062B/4659